From **Prison** to **Paycheck:**

What No One ever Tells You About Getting a Job

A Step-by-Step Guide

Pam Hogan

San Francisco, California

From Prison to Paycheck: What No On Ever Tells You About Getting a Job
A Step-by-Step Guide
by Pam Hogan

Publisher's Cataloging-in-Publication

Hogan, Pam. From prison to paycheck : what no one ever tells you about
getting a job : a step-by-step guide / Pam Hogan.
– 1st ed.
p.   cm.
Includes index.
LCCN 2007901679
ISBN-13: 978-0-9794294-9-1
ISBN-10: 0-9794294-9-8

1. Ex-convicts–Vocational guidance–United States.
2. Ex-convicts–Employment–United States.   3. Job hunting–United States.   I. Title.

HV9228.H64 2007   650.14'086927
                                                       QBI07-600158

Book design: Nick Zelinger, www.nzgraphics.com

Published by Community Press
P.O. Box 31667
San Francisco, CA 94131
888-739-2973

Orders@AcommunityPress.com
www.AcommunityPress.com

Printed in the United States of America

TABLE OF CONTENTS

INTRODUCTION

"Get a job," everyone tells you.

"You're going to need to find work right away," your parole officer says.

Obviously, it's important to get a job as quickly as possible because the sooner you do, the better your chances are for making it on the outside. The longer it takes to start earning money the legitimate way, the more tempting it is to make money the illegitimate way. And *that* can land you right back behind bars. It's no big secret.

You know there's no time to waste; but how do you go about getting a job? How do you perform an effective job search? Who can help you?

So many people get released from prison with the promise to themselves and others that they will go straight, that they will do it right, that they will get a job and give up the life that keeps landing them in prison. But something happens between the promise and the paycheck that derails the plan. And that something is reality.

The reality is you can have all of the best intentions to do something differently; but, if the knowledge is lacking, in the end you'll go for what you know.

Your doctor can tell you, for example, that if you don't lose weight you probably won't live to see your fiftieth birthday. You can promise your doctor that you'll lose weight, and deep down you can believe you will. But if you don't know how to lose that weight and how to keep it off, it really doesn't matter what you say or do. It doesn't matter at all that the consequences of ignoring his advice are so high. Sure, you might get lucky or someone might tell you what they did to lose weight. Their experience might work for you; then, again, it might not. If luck is all you have to count on, it doesn't matter if you're trying to lose weight or trying to find a job. It's unrealistic to expect success just because you *want* to be successful.

So, improve your odds; don't just hope Lady Luck will smile on you—it makes no sense to leave something so important to chance. Even without a record, there are dos and don'ts associated with a successful job search. With a criminal record, you have your very own set of special challenges that you absolutely must learn to navigate. If you have no training, no guidance, and no roadmap to help ensure success, the challenges are even worse.

Some people spend more time mapping out a trip than they do mapping out important aspects of their lives like securing employment. They head out without direction and quickly run into dead ends and roadblocks that convince them it's an impossible journey. What they don't realize is that, if they had had the right guidance, they could have had a totally different experience. So if you've tried in the past and you've failed, try again now that you're armed with a guide at your side.

Read this guide, study it, and refer back to it as needed, because it is the road map you need to succeed on your journey. It will point you in the right direction, show you where to head, and ultimately take you every step of the way. Because it assumes nothing, it explains everything. Once you've learned what's in the pages and sections to come, you'll know what it takes to hear those magic words: *"You're hired!"*

Don't waste another minute. Launch your journey right now—your job awaits.

Chapter 1

THE RESUME

Let's start with first things first. A company cannot consider you for a job unless you apply for that job. And the first step in applying for a job is to supply a calling card.

Imagine you're with a friend at the store, talking in the check-out line about the fact that you're looking for someone to do your taxes. At some point, the guy in front of you turns around and says, "Excuse me. I don't mean to intrude, but I couldn't help but overhear that you might be in need of my services. Allow me to give you my card." By receiving this person's card you now have everything you need to make a decision about him. You have his name. You have a way to contact him, since his phone number is on the card. His address, which is also on the card, lets you know he's close to where you live. The initials "CPA" beside his name tell you he's qualified for the job. And lastly, the line "Serving Your Financial Needs Since 1999" tells you that he has experience in the field. His business card has provided you with enough information to help you determine if you might want him to do your taxes.

When you're a person running a business, your business card is the item that simplifies an initial introduction; when you're a person conducting a job search, your resume serves that same purpose. A resume provides a company with your name, your contact information, your educational background, your skills, and your work history. A resume is the one item most commonly requested by employers (even the blue-collar industries). So, if you want a job, you need to have one. If you say you're looking for a job but you don't have a current resume, then you're not seriously looking for a job.

ADVANTAGES OF USING A RESUME

Resumes have taken over, in many places, where job applications left off. And, that's a good thing in many respects because they offer several advantages in your job search. Before resumes became the most commonly used means of applying for a job, you had to physically walk into every location where you wanted to apply and take the time to fill out an application. This was a time-consuming proposition. Today, most companies don't want to see you, or in many cases even speak with you, until they first look at your resume. You will either mail, fax, or e-mail your resume to a company, which means you can apply to far more companies in far less time.

Another advantage the resume has over applications is specific to someone with a criminal record, and this should make you a *huge* fan of the resume. Unlike an application, the resume does not disclose the fact that you've been convicted of a crime. When you submit a resume, your conviction will only be exposed, if at all, after you have been called in for an interview. The interview is a much stronger stage in the hiring process than the application stage, so it's a better time to have your conviction revealed. If the company doesn't care about your background, the question may not even come up at all.

TYPES OF RESUMES

There are three types of resumes.

- The resume that focuses on your work experience is called a chronological resume. This resume works well for people who have no gaps in their work history and whose strength is their extensive work experience.
- The functional resume, also called the skills resume, emphasizes the skills in your background rather than your work history.

> If you have jumped from field to field or if you have gaps in your work history or if you have no work history at all, this is the best type of resume for you.
- The hybrid, a combination of the chronological resume and the functional resume, is the third type of resume.

This book is written for the person who has spent time in prison and would have gaps in their work history, so the functional/skills resume is the only type of resume detailed in this book. (Keep in mind that, since the functional resume *is* often used to de-emphasize work history, some employers will see the functional resume as a red flag, signaling that an applicant is trying to hide something. For that reason, as your job history grows, you will want to shift your functional resume to more of a hybrid, at least until you can use the more common chronological format.) Most books you find for the general public focus on the chronological resume; it shouldn't be hard for you to develop a chronological resume using one of these books as a guide.

When it comes down to it, regardless of the type you use, an employer wants an attractive resume in an easy-to-read format that can be looked over quickly. *It's very important that you keep that in mind as you create your resume.* Doing so will enable employers to get a sense of you just by scanning the page. That's important because, with the number of resumes employers receive, you'll be competing for their time before you ever start competing for their job opening. Your resume must be easy for a reader to skim, and your skills must jump out at them. If something grabs their interest, they will read the details. If nothing jumps out to grab them, if they have to work to get a sense of what you bring to the table, they will likely set the resume aside. They may or may not ever return to it.

A resume, just like the business card discussed earlier, must present a professional image, and it must represent you in the best light possible, which means that even one grammatical error, typo, or misspelled word can hurt you. Also, like the business card, a resume is meant to whet the appetite of the reader not to tell your whole life story, which means it needs to be kept to one page, and one page only.

MAKING A STRONG DISPLAY

If you walked past a department store window and saw a set of free weights being displayed beside a weight bench, a treadmill, and a punching bag, you'd think nothing of the choice to combine those items in one display window. They all fall into the category of fitness equipment, and it makes sense for them to be shown together. If, however, you saw a display window with a weight bench, a baby crib, a ladder, and a nightgown, you'd probably scratch your head and wonder why anyone would display such very different items together in one window.

Since these items don't share a common relationship with each other, each item detracts from the other. Rather than looking at the display and saying, "Wow, they have something for everyone," you would probably question whether they could really meet your needs. After all, why would you expect to get a good weight-lifting set from a place that sells baby furniture and nightgowns? In fact, the store might be a *great* place for fitness equipment, but because of the display, you have some doubt.

Your resume is your very own display window. And just as one department store window can't be all things to all shoppers, your resume can't be all things to all positions. But, by making only a few simple yet key changes to your "window," your resume will become appropriate to each viewer.

The first step in getting your job search off to a good start is creating resume number one that you will continue to change for each new job title. With those changes, you will only display the skills and experiences appropriate to that particular job title. When employers view that resume, they will see you as a strong candidate with appropriate skills and experiences because they will see only what you have to offer for their particular opening.

This section will walk you step-by-step through the process of creating that all-important first resume. Whether you have lots of experience or you've never worked a day in your life, this chapter will guide you through creating resumes that make you shine.

To make it easy on yourself, take out a piece of paper right now so you can actively follow along when you come to the "Your Turn" directions. If you follow the instructions along the way, you'll have everything you need at the end of this section to head to a computer and type up your brand new resume.

OBJECTIVE

The first chance you get at making a good impression with a resume is the first line that follows your contact information. That line is the objective line (See Figure 1), and it simply states your objective—the position desired. The objective line sets the tone for the rest of the resume, kind of like the title of a book or the subject line in an e-mail. The objective line lets the reader know what to expect, what they're going to read next. If you use the objective line correctly, it will make your resume stronger; if you use it incorrectly, you might as well not use it at all.

The correct way to use an objective line is to briefly state the type of position you seek, like "Position as a delivery driver." The wrong way to use an objective line is to write something very generic, like "A position with room for advancement," which tells the reader nothing useful about you and your career goals.

Figure 1

Jaime Jones
222 Main Street
Colorado Springs, CO 80949
719-599-0987

OBJECTIVE: Entry level position as a custodian.

Notice in Figure 1 that Jaime uses the term "entry level," which means a position that doesn't require experience. Many companies are willing to hire someone to fill an entry level position and then train them from the bottom-up in exchange for paying low wages. It's a great way to get your foot in the door when you don't have experience in a field. When employers see that Jaime's objective is to get an entry level job as a custodian, they know right away not to expect to see a lot of custodial experience.

The objective line and the body of the resume should complement each other. If the objective Jaime lists is an entry level position, but then the body of the resume lists a lot of previous experience as a custodian, the reader will be left scratching his or her head, trying to understand why Jaime is seeking entry level work. Likewise, if Jaime's objective was to acquire a position in upper management, but the body of the resume didn't reflect any kind of supervisory experience the interviewer would be equally lost.

The objective line can talk the talk, but the body of your resume has to then walk the walk, or you'll confuse or possibly irritate your reader.

It's Your Turn

1. Think about what type of position you're looking for. You may have more than one position in mind, but for now just concentrate on one. (Once you finish resume number one, you can easily adapt it to make resumes for a second, third, or even fourth and fifth, position.)

2. Write the word "Objective" on a piece of paper followed by a colon.

3. Write down the position you thought about—just as you see in Figure 1.

EDUCATION

Where you place items on a resume is important. You want to place your strengths at center stage and your weaknesses in the background; you want to put the items most important to the position front and center, as well.

If, for example, you're trying to get a position involving computer repair, you would want the fact that you have *A+ Certification* (a part of your education) in computer repair to immediately follow your objective. If your education is not relevant to the job this resume is directed toward or if you do not have a four-year college degree, then you would want to position your education last on the page. If you don't have a high school diploma, a GED, or any formal or related education, then don't make a section for education on your resume at all. (If this *is* your situation, to help you with your job search, make it a point to enroll in a GED course so that you can list it on your resume.)

_____ *It's Your Turn* _____

1. Write "Education" on your paper.

2. If you have a GED, write the following using the city and state where you obtained it:

Education

General Educational Development Diploma, Denver, CO

If you *don't* have your GED *but you are taking classes* in an effort to obtain it, write:

Education

Currently enrolled in General Educational Development Diploma program
John Adams College, Baltimore, MD

3. If you have a high school diploma, write the following on your sheet using the name of the high school you attended:

Education

Diploma, Locke High School, Los Angeles, CA

4. If you have a certificate from a relevant program you've completed, list it under whatever other education you have listed:

Education

Diploma, Locke High School, Los Angeles, CA
Certified Welder, Metal Workers Institute, Atlanta, GA

5. If you have a high school diploma and you've taken some college classes, move your college information in front of your high school information. If you've attended one community college over the years list it by name or if you've attended several follow the example below.

Education

Community College, 3 years
Diploma, Locke High School, Los Angeles, CA

If you're currently attending a community college, write:

Education

Harbor College, Harbor City, CA, ongoing studies
Diploma, Locke High School, Los Angeles, CA

If you have taken a few college courses that relate specifically to the field you're applying for, it might be helpful to list that fact:

Education

Harbor College, Harbor City, CA, 12 units in welding
Diploma, Locke High School, Los Angeles, CA

Once you acquire a four year degree (a bachelor's degree), you no longer list your high school education.

Education

B.A., Social Welfare, Stanford University, Stanford, CA

Only list certificates that make sense for the position you're applying for. If you're applying for a customer service position, for example, listing your welding certificate won't make any sense for this particular resume; list the welding certificate on the resume you create for welding positions . . . remember the display window. Along those same lines, listing your drafting certificate and your welding certificate and your certificate in furniture upholstery all on one resume will make your work history appear like you've had a lot of false starts. That can lead an employer to wonder if this job is just one more false start. Again, think of your resume as a business card. You wouldn't want your new doctor handing you a card that said "Dr. Jones, Specialist in Pediatric Medicine and Car Detailing," would you?

One more thing to be cautious of when it comes to certificates: it's often best not to list certificates from organizations that help you with prisoner reentry or anger management or parenting classes. These certificates deserve a special place on your wall as they acknowledge your personal achievements, but a resume is not the place to list personal development work. Another good reason not to list them is that some agencies may be known as organizations that help people who have criminal records, which is information you don't want to disclose on a resume.

Finally, there is no need to list a date in your Education section unless (1) you will benefit in some way from an employer being able to guess your age, or (2) you are applying for your first job after graduating from high school or college. This tells an employer when your work history begins.

WORK HISTORY

It's now time to think back to the jobs you've had over the years. Another nice thing about a resume is that you don't have to recall exact addresses or phone numbers, the city and state will do just fine for location. (You should still track down this information for those companies that need an application on file; some still like applications since they do require more details than you will put on your resume.)

It's Your Turn

1. Write "Work History" on your paper.

2. List the job titles you have had, the most recent first.
   The older the job the farther down on the list it should appear.

3. Beside each title, write down the names of the companies you've worked for.

4. Beside the company's name, write down the city and state where they were located.

5. Add the year you started and the year you left to each line.

This section might look something like this:

Work History

Laborer	Mack & Sons Construction, Atlanta, GA	2005–2006
Security Guard	Security Network, Atlanta, GA	2003–2004
Stock Clerk	George's Grocers, Savannah, GA	1997–2000

If you are currently working at one of the jobs listed on your resume, you would write "present" in place of the date you left, for example, "2005–present." If you worked a job for less than a year, list only that one year once. For example, you would not write "2005–2005," only "2005," as shown below.

To list work with temporary agencies, follow this example:

Work History

Various Assignments	Manpower Temporary Agency, Atlanta, GA	2007–present
Laborer	Mack & Sons Construction, Atlanta, GA	2005
Security Guard	Security Network, Atlanta, GA	2003–2004
Stock Clerk	George's Grocers, Savannah, GA	1997–2000

An employer expects your work history to go back at least ten or fifteen years. (If you would have been a kid if you went back that far, only go back to your first job. If that is the case, remember to list the date you completed your education. This immediately tells an employer that you've gone back as far in your work history as is reasonably possible.) If you have accumulated a total of fifteen years of work history but you have a gap in your employment after your tenth year, stop your history at ten years rather than show the gap.

If you have a work history but the gaps in it are large and obvious all the way through it, you'll be better off using another format for dates on your resume. Rather than listing the years when you worked, tell the amount of time at each location. Try to list only jobs where you stayed for at least four months, preferably six. Below is an example:

Work History

Laborer	Mack & Sons Construction, Atlanta, GA	2 years
Security Guard	Security Network, Atlanta, GA	7 months
Stock Clerk	George's Grocers, Savannah, GA	1 year

If you jumped around a lot from one position to another, only staying a short time at each one but remaining in the same field, you would be better off combining the work into one listing. For example, rather than listing that you worked for four months at Security Network and seven months at ADT, you would look better to combine the two and round up the total time to twelve months, like this:

Work History

| Security Guard | ADT/Security Network, Atlanta, GA | 1 year |

If your resume screams "job jumper," you will have a hard time finding someone willing to take the chance that you're going to stick around awhile this time. Create a stronger resume by being smart about what you list, and how you list it. Combine similar positions, as shown above, and only list jobs that you held for at least six months. Then be sure to address the issue in your cover letter.

SKILLS SUMMARY

You're halfway finished! You have now completed your objective line and two of the four major components in your resume. It's time to tackle the Skills Summary section of the resume by recording the skills you've acquired while working.

Here is an easy way to think about your skills: Did you work with equipment, machinery, people, or paper? These are the essentials of functioning at a job, no matter what your position might have been. Some jobs require that you work with all four. Let's look at the skills you've learned and the best way to present them on your resume.

1. Equipment

Equipment refers to the tools needed to accomplish a task—everyday items like shovels, mops, shampooers, waxers, buffers, brooms, lawn mowers, and nail guns are considered equipment. But because these are such common tools, and because they don't require extensive, special training to use them, it's better not to list them by name on a resume. It's best to list these sorts of items collectively as "light equipment," like this:

Skills Summary
Use of light equipment.

Think back to the business card model . . . you would find it silly to read on a gardener's card that they could use a lawn mower. On the other hand, to know they could use an aerial lift to prune your trees *would* be something to note as a selling point. Similarly, if you know how to use a forklift, a back-hoe, a tractor, or a crane—items that require special training—it would benefit you to list that equipment by name.

So, to start your skills summary section, if you are skilled in anything that required training, *something the average person wouldn't be expected to know how to use*, list that piece of equipment by name followed by the word "operation."

Skills Summary
Crane operation.
Forklift operation.

2. Machinery

Apply the same line of thinking to machinery. Avoid listing common items like copiers or fax machines by combining them into one phrase: "Proficient in the use of all office machines." But, if you know how to use a machine that a person walking in off the street could not use without training, list that machine by name. Beside these names, describe the level of your skills as honestly as possible by using the following terms:

- "Proficient" means you're highly skilled in using that piece of machinery.
- "Competent" means you are only sufficiently skilled at using it.
- Having a "working knowledge of" a machine means you're not skilled in the machine's use, but you know your way around it.
- Being "familiar with" a machine means just that—you're familiar with the machine, but you may not have experience using it.

_____ *It's Your Turn* _____

1. Add the heading "Skills Summary" to your paper.

2. If you have experience with common tools that don't require extensive, special training to use, group them collectively as "light equipment" and enter the following line under the heading: "Use of light equipment."

Skills Summary
Use of light equipment.

3. If you are skilled in anything that required training, list that piece of equipment and add the word "operation" after it.

Skills Summary
Tractor operation.
Crane operation.

4. List the names of machines you can use. If you can primarily use general office machines like copiers and fax machines, just add "Proficient in the use of all office machines." If you have had to have training to use a machine, list that machine by name. Following the name, describe the level of your skills—as honestly as possible—by using the terms discussed above.

Skills Summary

Use of light equipment.
Proficient in the use of all office machines.
Working knowledge of Sharp XE-A404 Electronic Cash Register.
Familiar with offset printing.

3. People

An often overlooked skill is the one that's required to work effectively with people. A business can be extremely good at what it does, but if customers hate going there because of the way they're treated, it can negatively impact the success of the business. If you have the ability to work well with people, you have a skill that deserves mention on your resume. Again, you have to use the correct terms to give that skill the weight and value it deserves:

- If it's customers you're good with, refer to that talent as having good "customer relations."
- If you work well with co-workers, you have good "interpersonal relations," or you have the ability to be a "team player."
- If you've managed people, you have "leadership skills," "management skills," or "supervisory skills."
- If you can show people how to do things and they understand you well enough to do it themselves, you have "teaching skills," or "training skills."
- If you have listened to a client explain what they need and have directed them to take a certain action based on that conversation, you have "consulting skills."
- If you have done in-store demonstrations or given talks at your church or other functions, you have "presentation skills," "public speaking skills," or "communication skills."
- If you have sold things over the telephone, you have "telemarketing skills."
- If you are comfortable working with different ethnic groups or age groups or people of various sexual orientations, you are "skilled in working with diverse groups."

- If you work well without supervision, or without someone checking up on you regularly, and you take the initiative to get things done, you're a "self-starter."

_____ *It's Your Turn* _____

Give some thought to the people skills you have and add them to the skills summary section of your page. Use the discussion above and the list below to help with your choices.

Skills Summary

Excellent customer relations skills.
Strong management skills.
Highly effective interpersonal relations skills.
Outstanding leadership and supervisory skills.
Effective telephone skills.
Comfortable and effective working with diverse populations.
Strong teaching skills.
Friendly and effective consulting skills.
Superior conflict management skills.
Good communication skills.
Effective public speaker and overall good communicator.
Team player.
Self-starter.

4. Paper

The last category for which you may have skills falls under the heading of paper, or paperwork. Have you handled paperwork before? Completed reports? Filed? Catalogued or organized papers of any kind?

It's hard to do any kind of work for a company without also having to keep some kind of paper trail, even if it was just a driver's log. Think of these skills in terms of doing it right, doing it on time, and catching your own mistakes. Use the term "accurate" to describe completing or handling paperwork correctly. If you get things done on time then you do them in a "timely manner," or you "meet deadlines." If you tend to look for and catch your own mistakes before calling the job done, then you have "attention to detail." Think of how you handle paperwork and apply the appropriate description to best describe your skills in this category. Add your decisions to your list of skills.

<u>Skills Summary</u>

Strong attention to detail.
Accurate and timely in report submission.
Extremely organized and thorough.
Excellent follow-through skills.
Attentive to deadlines.

AN ADDITIONAL NOTE ABOUT PEOPLE AND PAPER

The skills from the people and paper sections have a special name—they're known as "soft skills." Soft skills have nothing to do with the technical knowledge or the expertise a job requires (those are actually called "hard skills"). Instead, soft skills have more to do with personality traits and can be applied to any number of jobs.

When it comes to soft skills, it doesn't matter how you got them. These are skills reflected in your personality and your character. Some of us are just born as leaders, have always been good communicators, are well-organized by nature—it's just a part of who we are. Employers don't care that your excellent ability to follow through on a project came about as a result of being raised by an alcoholic mother who left you to fend for yourself. They won't care that your leadership skills come from all the times you headed up a basketball game. Nor will they care if you're good with customers because you once sold drugs, where you learned to finesse the clientele to keep them happy.

When it comes to soft skills, employers are looking for a different side of your story. Rather than focusing on how you came to have a particular soft skill, an employer wants to know how you have used that skill in the workplace, or, better yet, how you will use the skill in the potential position. But, we'll be addressing presentation of your skills later.

You may have a very long list of both soft and hard skills in your Skills Summary section after thinking in terms of equipment, machinery, people, and paper. To create the most concise and effective resume possible, you need to find the *five* skills that you would use the most in the job you're applying for, since they will be the most appealing to an employer skimming your resume. This section needs to be reviewed each time you create a resume with a new objective to make sure you have the best five skills listed for the position.

It's Your Turn

1. Look at your objective and your skills summary and think about which skills an employer would like most to see from an applicant who has that objective listed.

2. With this in mind, number the hard skill *best* suited for the position with a one. Find the second best hard skill suited for the position and number it with a two, and so on until you have ranked the hard skills that are the best match for the position from one to five.

3. If you were able to find five hard skills that match the position you are finished with this section; if not, look among your soft skills and continue numbering until you reach five.

4. If you have no hard skills at all for this position then fill this section with soft skills only, but reduce the number to four. As with the hard skills, rank your soft skills in order of their strength.

RELEVANT EXPERIENCE

Your sheet now has an objective line, your educational background, your work history, and your skills summary. You are just about finished. You only have one major category left.

The last section you're going to write focuses on relevant work experience. Although you have gained some experience from each job you've worked at, the section you are about to create is titled "Relevant Experience" because it only contains experience that relates to the position you're applying for. The last thing an employer wants to do is wade through everything you've ever done at every job you've ever had to find the experience best suited for the position you're applying for. As discussed earlier, your resume must grab the reader with just a glance and a skim, and the Relevant Experience section plays a big part in making such a reader-friendly resume possible. This section is where you really need to be smart about what you display in your window. Make sure you don't have a "weight bench" next to a "baby bed" by listing things that don't fit with your objective.

It's Your Turn

1. Write "Relevant Experience" as the next heading on your sheet.

2. Underneath, describe the major duties you performed at each job you listed in the "Work History" section. Describe the task as a whole so as to avoid detailing each aspect of an activity. For example, "Cleaned 50 offices a day." is preferred over "Dusted furniture, emptied garbage cans, and vacuumed offices." Also, be sure to use the past tense.

3. When you finish writing these job descriptions, look at your objective line again, then go back and circle the descriptions that relate best to your objective. For example, if your objective is "Position as a busboy," then you'll circle the duties that have something to do with the food industry or cleaning.

Here's a good example of what this section should look like:

Relevant Experience
Stocked incoming merchandise on a daily basis.
Tracked all inventory in the store.
Created displays for sale items.
Kept shelves clean and presentable for customers.

You can guess the position this person might be applying for just by reading the items listed in this section, can't you? That's the idea. If the objective is not obvious when you read your list, then you need to tighten it up.

This section will change, probably more than any other, as you create additional resumes with different objectives for different positions you're applying for. You'll need to change this section to match any new objective, whenever it changes.

UNDERSTANDING THE FORMAT

Figure 2 shows you what your page should now look like in the correct order and format and with the proper headings. The sections are arranged in order of importance to the reader so as to deliver the biggest impact possible with a skim of the page.

Once employers note your objective, their eyes will scan your skills summary and your relevant experience to see if you have what they're looking for. (Notice how the bullets in the Relevant Experience section set these items apart. In most cases, if you're using a recent version of Microsoft Word, a popular word-processing program, you will see the icon for inserting bullets right on the toolbar.)

Work history follows next because if employers like what they've seen in the first two sections, they'll then want to see where you acquired your experience. They'll look to your work history for that. This section will also tell them a few other things, like how long you tend to stay in one position, and whether you have gaps in your work history.

Finally, they will notice your Education section. If, on the other hand, an ad has mentioned a specific educational requirement they'll be looking for this early in their initial scan. If this is the case, and you meet this educational requirement, position your education beneath your Objective line as discussed earlier.

Figure 2

Chris Smith
222 Broad Street
New York, NY 10121
212-999-0999

OBJECTIVE: Position as a stock clerk.

SKILLS SUMMARY

Use of light equipment.
Strong attention to detail.
Extremely organized and thorough.
Excellent follow through.

RELEVANT EXPERIENCE

- Stocked incoming merchandise on a daily basis.

- Tracked all inventory in the store.

- Created displays for sale items.

- Kept shelves clean and presentable for customers.

WORK HISTORY

Laborer	Mack & Sons Construction, Atlanta, GA	2005–2007
Security Guard	Security Network, Atlanta, GA	2004
Stock Clerk	George's Grocers, Savannah, GA	2000–2001

EDUCATION

Diploma, Locke High School, Los Angeles, CA

CONGRATULATIONS!

Good work. If you've been following along, you now have in front of you a completed, handwritten resume. Using this resume as a model, you will be able to create several strong resumes. Can you see how easy it will be for you to make only a few deletions, a couple of additions, and some minor changes to have, in a matter of minutes, a second or third resume for other positions you might be interested in?

Now that you have your first resume composed, you're also ready for one more tip that will enhance your resume and give you an edge over your competition. When you read an ad that mentions a certain skill, and you possess that skill, make sure to list it at the top of your Skills Summary section if it isn't already there. By doing so, the first thing the employer sees is that you have the exact skill (or skills) they're looking for.

For example, you may read an ad for a busboy position that says, "Hectic downtown restaurant looking for busboy." Ask yourself, *What kind of person would I have to be to work well in a hectic restaurant?*

For one thing, you probably thought that you'd have to be able to work well under pressure. If this sounds like you, then you want to list that skill at the top of the Skills Summary section: "Ability to work well under pressure." This required nothing more than adding one line to your resume, but the benefit can be huge. By telling employers, right up front, that you have the skills they listed or hinted at in their ad, they can't help but feel like you're just what they're looking for.

By the way, you've probably already noticed this, but to make it "official," here is one of the most important rules of resume writing: The appropriate way to phrase things on a resume (and, this may take some getting used to) is in simple terms and in a list. For example, you should never use the word "I" or the phrase "I have (the)." You say "Ability to work well under pressure," not "*I have the* ability to work well under pressure." Write "Strong people skills," not "I have strong people skills." State "Ability to work as a team player," not "I have the ability to work as a team player." Using "I" or "I have (the)" is one of the biggest no-nos in resume writing. Think of looking at a resume and seeing "I have . . ." "I have . . ." "I have . . ." "I have . . ." running in a straight line all the way down the page—wouldn't that be irritating?

TYPING IT UP

Now that you've written out your resume, you're ready to type it into a computer.

- Be consistent with your formatting. For example, it would be distracting to see one job title in bold and another one underlined. The same goes for spacing—keep it consistent, usually single-spaced for information lines and double-spaced between headings.
- "Font face" is the style of print used. You want to use a font face that is commonly used for professional purposes, like Times New Roman, which is typically the default you'll find in a word-processing program before you change anything. Arial is another font face that is nice for professional purposes.
- "Font size" determines how large or small the print is; you should use 12 point. Don't increase your font size to take up more space, but decrease your font size to 11 or 10 point if that's what it takes to fit your resume on one page. Do not make it smaller than 10 point.
- To correctly abbreviate a state, use post office abbreviations and capitalize both letters with no periods. For example, *Georgia* is no longer abbreviated as "Ga."; "GA" should be used instead.
- Remember that job titles, whether a doctor or a desk clerk, are not capitalized when used in an ordinary sentence. However, they are capitalized under Work History because of the format of that section. So, in your objective line and your cover letters, you would not capitalize job titles, but you would capitalize them in your Work History section.
- In the Skills Summary section, pay attention to the adjectives, the descriptive words, that you use before a skill. You want to make sure that you don't use the same adjective three or four times. It won't look very creative if you say "Strong communication skills," "Strong telephone skills," "Strong customer relations skills," . . .
- Don't spend extra money having your resume printed on fancy paper; it's not necessary.

When you have your first resume just the way you want it, save it using your name and position, for example "Denise Newman Driving Position." Then, immediately, use the "Save As" function to save the resume with a new name. Use an appropriate name for that next resume—for example, "Denise Newman Janitor Position." Now you can make whatever changes you need to without the fear of accidentally changing something on your original resume. When naming your resume, it's always a good idea to use your name and the position you're applying for. That makes it easier for an employer to match it up with your cover letter if you've been asked to apply via e-mail.

Make sure you keep all of your resumes up to date as you add new skills and work experience.

If your computer skills prevent you from being able to create a resume or from making necessary changes or performing the tasks described in this section, you may want to join www.HelpAfterPrison.com. For a small monthly fee, this membership Web site for previously incarcerated individuals provides unlimited access to training modules on the many skills needed to be successful in the working world, including computer literacy. You can access all of the training modules twenty-four hours a day (and as many times as you need to) to learn various skills.

"BUT I'VE NEVER WORKED A DAY IN MY LIFE"

If you have never held a legitimate job and your resume is basically a skills summary without a work history or with only a very brief one (such as, you're working right now and it's the only job you've ever had), then you need to address this in your objective line. This is one way to address it:

"Objective: To enter the workforce in an entry level driving position."

You accomplish two things by stating your objective this way. First, you acknowledge the obvious lack of work history by using the phrase "to enter the workforce." Second, you show that you're willing to start from the bottom by seeking an "entry level" position.

You need to also find a way to acknowledge your lack of work history in your cover letter. Something to the effect of, "Although a late bloomer, I have a strong aptitude for janitorial work" then continue to sell your skills as discussed in the chapter on cover letters.

FINAL WORDS

You now have the tools to create the strongest resumes possible by customizing them to fit each position you apply for while using a format that will emphasize your strengths. This is a skill you will use for the rest of your working life.

If you followed this chapter closely, you will have created the type of resumes that will get you interviews. Reread the chapter if anything seems fuzzy; it's amazing what will become clearer the second time around. If you still need help after reading and rereading the chapter, take what you've created to a career counselor (someone you might find at the employment office) or to a nonprofit organization that works with functional resume preparation. It might be helpful to show them a copy of Figure 2 so they're aware of the format you're using. They should be able to get you the rest of the way.

Chapter 2

THE JOB SEARCH

Looking for a job needs to be taken seriously. It's a full-time job itself, and it needs to be approached with the same work ethic as if it were a paying job. Just as you wouldn't sleep in late, handle personal business, play with your kids, or watch television if you were working a nine-to-five job, you shouldn't use your daytime hours in this way when you're looking for a job, either. Your work day is at least from 9:00 to 4:00 when you're looking for work, which means you need to be up, showered, and ready for "work" at 9:00. Some companies only accept job applications or take phone calls in the morning. If *your* morning starts in the afternoon you'll miss out on these opportunities.

Of course, getting up in the morning also prepares you for the day when you *will* be working. You don't want to have to wage an internal battle between the part of you that sincerely wants to find a job and the part of you that's gotten hooked on daytime television or enjoys sleeping in. You have to stay in job search mode, which means keeping your head in the game every day of the week, from 9:00 to 4:00. It takes a good work ethic to hold a job, and it takes a good work ethic to get a job. Every minute of every day that you use your daytime hours on something other than your job search postpones your success. Schedule doctor's appointments, or any other kind of unrelated business, as close to the end of the day as possible.

Survey data show that many people fail to get jobs because they just don't look hard enough. And, since you're three times more likely to go back to prison if you don't have a job, you definitely do not want to be one of those not looking hard enough. So, get your head in the game and keep it there until you hear the words, "You're hired!"

That said, what is a day in the life of someone seriously looking for work like? Your day should go something like this . . .

THE INTERNET

Gone are the days when the Sunday newspaper listed all the newest ads and by Wednesday all those leads were gone. The Internet makes new online employment ads available several times a day and you should make a point of checking them as frequently as you possibly can.

If you are using a location outside of the house to access online ads, like an employment agency or the library, leave the house professionally dressed, armed with resumes that are placed in something that will keep them fresh and unfolded.

So, let's talk about using the Internet for your job search. If you're not familiar with the Internet, take a free class at a local library or at the employment office or community college in some cases, or wherever a free class of this kind would be taught in your city. If possible, take an Internet class that's geared toward job seekers because it will also introduce you to useful Web sites that are specific to job searching. If you cannot locate a formal class, ask a librarian for help getting started with an online job search. They will get you up to speed in no time. (Talking to a librarian is not a bad idea even if you find a class, since every area tends to have its own, best go-to sites for job searching, and librarians often know those sites.) The library will also have a number of books that provide ideas for Internet job searching. In fact, there's a book that seems to get updated regularly called exactly that: *Guide to Internet Job Searching*. It's written by Margaret Riley Dikel and Frances E. Roehm. (You should also spend some time with Appendix 1 in the back of this book because it lists useful job search sites for each state.)

Once you're comfortable using the Internet, one fantastic Web site for job hunting is www.craigslist.com. The site doesn't have listings for every city in the country, so go to the site and click on your state to see if you find your city. If you're lucky enough that your city is listed, explore all of the various categories first thing so you know what types of jobs can be found where.

When using a job search site, after you've explored the categories and scanned the listings, it's often helpful to do keyword searches. For example, if you want to only find entry level positions, you would type "entry level" into the keyword search box, and the resulting list will provide all of the jobs that contain the words "entry level" in their ads. If you have little or no work experience, then searching for entry level positions will save you time. You can also do a keyword search for the type of work you're looking for—for example, "busboy," "driver," "customer service," "janitor," or "roofer," and you will only get ads for those positions. This can be a big time saver, especially when using large databases.

By the way, be cautious about putting a lot of time into posting a resume online. This rarely returns much result for the effort, especially when you're not in a field that's in high demand and you have limited skills to advertise.

READING ADS

Whether you read them online or in print, it will be helpful to know the different job titles and categories your fields of interest might fall under in listings. For example, "hospitality" refers to work in the hotel industry, even though, at first glance, you might think it referred to work in hospitals. Janitors are also called custodians and ads for this type of work might fall under the category of "facilities maintenance." Also, don't confuse "survey taker" with "surveyor." Surveyors don't stand on the corner taking surveys; they typically work for an engineering company surveying land. Security guards are in the field of "loss prevention." Familiarity with these and similar terms will also help you during your interviews and with writing your cover letters.

Here are some other terms that you might find helpful:

- An ad that says it's looking for "independent contractors" is referring to the fact that you will not be an employee of the company. You will basically be acting as a self-employed person. That means you will have to pay your own taxes because they will not be deducted from your paycheck. It also means you won't get any employee benefits, like health insurance, because you're not an employee, that you'll do the work with little or no training, and you'll have to use your own tools and equipment in most cases. One advantage of being an independent contractor is that you usually create your own schedule and you usually have little direct supervision. You will often see this in sales ads and ads for driving positions.

- "Telemarketers," or "telefundraisers," are positions that often don't require experience as much as a willingness to sit on a phone all day "dialing for dollars," as they call it. A telemarketer sells things on the phone. A telefundraiser solicits for donations to raise funds. A telefundraiser usually works for a nonprofit organization calling on its membership base to request that they donate money to the organization. When you see the word "auto-dial" in the ad it refers to the fact that the company uses a computer to do automatic dialing for you so you don't have to "manually" dial.

- When you come across an ad where the company describes itself as a "start-up company," it means the company has only recently been formed and is probably still in the early stages of building a name for itself. When you see "well established company," you know you're dealing with the opposite.

- When you see "clean DMV req'd" in an ad, usually in ads for a driver or a delivery person, it means the company needs your driving record to be free from moving violations or any other negative marks. They will usually require you to obtain a computer printout of your driving record from the Department of Motor Vehicles (DMV) before they will seriously consider you for the position.

When reading ads, there are some concepts you should be aware of.

First, there's nothing more frustrating than getting excited about an ad you've found only to get down to the qualifications and find out you don't have the right experience or education. One way to avoid this disappointment when reading ads is to scan the bottom of the ad, where qualifications are typically listed, before you read anything else. This can help you save time and avoid frustration.

In addition, when it comes to qualifications, you should understand the difference between some key terms. An ad that says a certain skill, educational background, or amount of experience is *preferred* or *helpful* is very different from an ad that says a certain skill, educational background, or amount of experience is *required*. If it's "preferred" or "helpful," it means you still have a chance of being considered for that job, even if you don't have the listed skill, educational background, or amount of experience.

When an ad uses the words "experience required" or "college degree required" or notes that knowledge of a certain piece of equipment or machine is required, then you're probably wasting your time if you don't have it. Still, some companies will substitute your lack of education for a lot of experience in the field. For example, an ad might read "bachelor's degree preferred or equivalent experience is accepted" or it might be more specific and say the kind of experience and amount they feel is equal to the education requirement, so be sure to read the ad closely in these cases.

Next, if an ad says "no phone calls," do not spend time searching to uncover the company's number so you can call. You'll just be shooting yourself in the foot. Hiring managers are annoyed, not impressed, by this. You need to make sure you do whatever the ad says. If it requests you apply via e-mail then apply by sending information by e-mail; if it says to fax your resume, then fax it; if it tells you to call between 9 a.m. and 11 a.m., don't call at 2 p.m. Irritating people by disobeying or being inconsiderate to their request is not the way to get off to a good start.

In addition, be aware that some industries set certain times of day for accepting applications and may interview you on the spot. Remember, "game on" from the moment you leave the house—you just never know who you'll run into throughout the day or what opportunities will arise.

WALKING AND TALKING

First of all, it's important to realize that not all companies run ads when they have a position they want to fill. If they're located in a neighborhood that gets a lot of foot traffic some businesses simply put a "Help Wanted" sign in the window and save the expense and effort of running ads. Other companies don't advertise because, to some extent, they're always hiring at one location or another, so they accept applications on an ongoing basis. This allows them to maintain a pool of applicants to choose from. By walking into establishments and asking if they're accepting applications, and by staying on the look-out for "Help Wanted" signs you will expand your job search to include companies you may not otherwise reach. Make sure before you go into an establishment that you have the appropriate resume at the front of your stack so you don't have to thumb through the pile to get the one that's best suited for that type of company. You want to appear organized and on the ball. Once again, the importance of being dressed in business attire for this strategic walk cannot be stressed enough.

Now, then, it's time to take the walking to another level. Besides watching out for signs and interesting businesses while you walk, stay on the lookout for people wearing uniforms or driving company vehicles. Make it a point to ask if their company is hiring. If they say, "Yes," ask who would be the best person to talk to about applying. Try to get the name of the person who handles applications so that when you call the company, you're not just asking for the manager or the personnel office or the human resources department—you're asking for someone by name. Try, also, to get the name of the person you're talking with.

When you get home you will make cold calls to these companies. (Calling someone you don't know in an effort to acquire information or sell something is called "cold calling.") When you call and get connected with the appropriate person, don't ask if they have any openings, instead say,

> "Hi, Tina; this is John Smith. I'm calling because I spoke with William while he was running his route the other day, and he thought I should give you a call about some hiring you're going to be doing."

If she says, that, as far as she knows, they're not doing any hiring right now, your response should be,

> "Oh, really? He sure seemed to think so. Do you know if maybe he was thinking about a different department or maybe something in the warehouse?"

She might then turn you over to the manager of another department, just to be on the safe side. After all, some managers like to handle hiring directly and independently of the human resources department. If that's the case, you would give basically the same speech to the person she connects you to:

> "Hi, Michael; this is John Smith. I'm calling because I ran into William the other day on his route and, after talking briefly with Tina, it seems you're the best person for me to talk to about some hiring you may be doing. Is that right?"

During the work week, look at everyone you run into as if they have something you want—because they likely do! Not everyone is going to know if their company is hiring, but they will all know who you should talk to to find out. So, when you see the guy delivering water to an office building, the woman writing parking tickets, the person watering plants at the dentist's office, the guy picking up mats at the bakery, the lady dropping off auto parts at the mechanic shop—these people all have something you can get just for the asking. They all have the name and phone number of the person you should talk to where they work.

> "Excuse me, I was wondering, can you tell me who I would talk to at your company about employment?"
> "Oh, that would be Veronica."
> "Veronica, great. Could you give me a phone number?"
> "Yeah, its 777-9898."
> "Thanks a lot. I really appreciate that. What's your name?
> "J.R."
> "Thanks a lot, J.R. Have a good one."

When taking your strategic walks, be smart about how you use your time. For example, don't waste your time walking in areas that have only retail stores if you're more interested in getting a job working in an office or doing construction. Start walking at different places and in different directions so you always have new neighborhoods to cover. If you use public transportation to get to where you access the Internet, get off a stop or two early and walk to the employment office or the library. Or go a stop or two past the location and walk back. Walk in the neighborhood of your second bus if you have a connecting line to catch. You might even want to try a different employment office or library once in a while so that you get into different neighborhoods.

Before you head back home, go back to the place where you access the Internet and check the online ads again. (Remember, a three or four hour gap between checking online sites should be plenty of time to find a set of new ads waiting for you.)

Make a point of getting home early enough to make your cold calls on the leads you got throughout the day using the technique above. Don't save them until morning, because you need to be out of the house in the morning to start the process all over again.

SUPPORT AGENCIES AND NONPROFITS

To have a well-balanced approach to a job search, you have to have all of your irons in the fire. You want to be using online sources of job listings, you want to be using the above technique to cold call companies, you want to be walking neighborhoods. You want to be checking the classified section of the daily newspapers in your area, as well as looking in the smaller publications published less frequently—sometimes smaller companies that don't want to spend a lot of money running ads in the bigger papers will place cheaper ads in the papers that are free to the public. (You need to scrutinize these ads a little more closely, however, to make sure they're listing legitimate jobs and not trying to (1) sign you up for some kind of multi-level marketing program (2) sell you a directory for work-at-home jobs or (3) enroll you in a vocational training program.) These publications offer you a chance to connect with smaller companies where it is sometimes easier to get hired.

In addition to those sources, you already know to utilize agencies, like the employment office, that help people acquire jobs and organizations that specifically help people who have been incarcerated. But, you may also want to take advantage of agencies that help other groups, such as the homeless or those with low-incomes. (Note: Many of these organizations require that you participate in a class designed to provide you with job readiness skills. These classes can be very helpful and can provide useful information. This training is often one of the qualities employers appreciate about hiring people sent from such organizations.)

If you come across an organization that sounds like it only serves one population of people, inquire as to whether that's really the case. For example, Jewish Vocational Services and Catholic Charities help *anyone* in need of their services, not just Jews or Catholics. Besides offering assistance, nonprofit organizations often hire people who have a background similar to the population they serve. For example, agencies that work with the homeless, with substance abuse programs, with transitional housing, with prisoner reentry training, or with welfare-to-work programs are inclined to hire people who have experienced those conditions. You'll find a category for non-profit jobs on most job Web sites. One Web site specifically dedicated to displaying jobs for the nonprofit sector is www.opportunityknocks.org.

Another place to look is with business owners who have establishments located in neighborhoods that serve a population of people where you might be of service—for example, businesses in low income neighborhoods or residential hotels. Your time in prison makes you a better candidate for working with the clientele at a residential hotel than someone with more experience working in a posh hotel, where rooms cost $200 a night. That person probably wouldn't last a day in a residential hotel, but *you* would. Your past can be a strength, a skill, and a selling point, so make it a point to call on these types of establishments and build relationships with the owners. Make a point to stop by when you're professionally dressed.

NETWORKING

The idea behind networking is letting everybody you know and all of their friends know that you're looking for a job. Some people were lucky enough to have started networking the day they were born, and they're probably still in touch with the doctor that delivered them! For others, the only people in their network are people they would stop knowing if they knew what was good for them. (If you fall into this latter category, you have a disadvantage that you need to correct.)

Networking is an aspect of job hunting that you shouldn't ignore, and here are two reasons why this is the case. First, you can often find out about positions that are about to open up—yes, *before* they are advertised. Second, when you've been recommended to an employer by someone they already know and like and respect, you are in a far stronger position than other potential candidates.

It's important, therefore, to make sure that every employed adult in your social circle knows you're looking for work. This is not the time to let pride or shame get in your way. After all, this is how it's done in the professional world on a regular basis, so you should take advantage of this approach, as well. Don't just ask, "Hey man, are they hiring down at your job?" and accept an answer from someone who may have nothing to do with hiring. Instead ask, "Can you ask your boss if there are any positions about to open up that you may not know about?" A real friend should have no trouble looking into this for you. If you find out there is an opening, ask the friend to put in a good word for you, to see if they can get you in for an interview, or to find out what you need to do to help you get your foot in the door.

Networking should not stop at your friends. Think about networking in terms of people on the street—odds are good that at least one of them has heard of some place that's hiring. Take the guy at the liquor store, for instance. Wouldn't you kick yourself if you hadn't told him you were looking for work, then, one day, later, when you mention it casually in conversation, he says, "Wow, I wish I had known that last month. My cousin was looking for help at his deli." We tend to make friends with like-minded people, or at least to associate with them on occasion; meaning, business owners tend to know other business owners. Remember, networking extends beyond the people you know to the people *they* know, so don't limit yourself.

Make it easy on people to remember you by getting some inexpensive business cards printed. A business card will be retained longer than a piece of paper that doesn't say much. Online, you can get free business cards at www.vistaprint.com; they only charge for shipping and handling, which tends to be about $5. These cards can be nice and simple, with just your name, phone number, and e-mail address, and then a line that describes the type of work you're looking for. Something like, "Actively Seeking Employment in Facilities Maintenance;" or "Roofer Seeking Employment" will help jog the memories of the people you give cards to (especially when they're trying to remember why they have it five weeks down the road). You can even post your cards at coffee houses and other places that have bulletin boards for postings.

One final suggestion is to make a point of visiting the community college in your city and in all cities where you're willing to work. They usually have career centers, and although it's doubtful that you'll be able to utilize their counseling services if you're not a student, at the very least, you can look over the "Help Wanted" flyers that are posted at the center and in plain sight around campus.

JOB FAIRS

Another reason for visiting community colleges is to find out about job fairs in the area, which are often promoted on college campuses. You'll also want to keep an eye out for advertisements in the employment section of the newspaper, watch for flyers at the employment office, and listen for messages on the radio.

Job fairs are important avenues for job hunters because you have the chance to meet a lot of employers at one time; nothing compares to this opportunity to talk to so many company representatives in one day. Job fairs usually take place at a hotel or some place comparable in size. Numerous companies participate in job fairs and they have one reason for attending:

they're recruiting for positions they need to fill. Company representatives staff the tables and are usually eager to talk to interested attendees and answer questions. Often, you can leave behind a resume, so take several of the various types of resumes you have in your arsenal.

Besides taking lots of resumes, when you attend a job fair, dress professionally and work to make an impression. Don't treat the company representatives like they're vendors at a flea market by casually browsing, picking up literature without making eye contact, and waiting for them to make the first move. Make a good and memorable impression by acting as if you're speaking to an interviewer.

Ask questions like, "What positions are you recruiting for today?" "What kind of work experience is required for this position?" "What educational background is required for this position?" If the position seems like something you're interested in and qualified for, ask for a business card and see if you can leave a resume. Thank the person for their time, and shake hands before you walk away from their table. Then, be sure to make a note on the back of the business card you pick up to help you recall the person, the position, and the conversation.

You may be lucky enough to attend a job fair intended for individuals with criminal records. These are the very best to attend because you *know* the employers are open to hiring previously incarcerated individuals. Another place to find an entire list of employers open to hiring men and women with records is at the membership Web site mentioned earlier, www.HelpAfterPrison.com.

Keep in mind that your aim at a job fair is *not* to get offered a job right then and there. It just doesn't happen that way. Your goal is to connect with as many employers as possible, to make as many good impressions as you can, and to leave behind some fresh clean resumes.

THANK YOU LETTERS

This next step is key in helping you to make the most out of a job fair. As soon as you get home, mail out a thank you letter to the people you spoke with who had a position you were interested in. This gesture will help you to stand out from the crowd of people they met that day. Some people will call, some will e-mail, others will do no follow-up at all. But an actual thank you *letter*, mailed the old fashioned way, will definitely make you stand out. Keep the letter simple, the last thing you want is to do more harm than good with the follow-up letter. Make sure you don't sound desperate or like you're begging or pleading for work—those are pathetic turn-offs and they only hurt your cause.

Using the business letter format discussed in the next chapter on cover letters, write something along the lines of:

Dear Dwight:

Thank you for your time at the job fair today. It was a pleasure meeting you. I was very happy to hear that D&L Couriers is looking for drivers.

Per our conversation, I would love an opportunity to put my three years of driving experience and my clean driving record to good use with D&L. I look forward to hearing from you on the matter.

Enclosed for your convenience, please find another copy of my resume. Again, thank you for your time today.

Sincerely,

David Ross

If you made a connection that would help the person remember you then mention it. For the best effect, add a postscript, or a "P.S.," two lines after your name. For example,

P.S. It was a pleasure meeting another Laker's fan.

By including another resume, you do three very good things for yourself.

1. You prevent the need for the reader to look for your resume in the stack they are trying to get through.

2. You move your resume to the top of the pile because it's in the recruiter's hand right at that moment.
3. When they come across your first resume later, it will be familiar to them.

That makes three very good reasons to enclose a resume. To be effective, you need to get the thank you letter in the mail as soon as you get home. You want it to be received the next day or the day after.

GET ORGANIZED, KEEP TRACK, AND SET GOALS

As you can see, looking for a job is full-time work, and, if you're doing it right, you should be so busy that once you start working, you'll feel like you're on a vacation! You have to be out there consistently—making contacts, following up on leads, making notes so you remember when someone tells you to check back later. Some people, when they're told to check back with a company in two months, convince themselves that they'll be working in two months, and they don't hold on to the contact information. Sadly, three months later, they find themselves regretting that they were so short-sighted. Don't make that mistake. Stay organized. Create a job binder, a folder that has a bunch of pockets in it, so you can keep track of leads, future call backs, business cards, ads you've responded to, and everything else relevant to your job search.

You need to keep track of what you've sent but you also need to quickly forget about what you've sent. If you begin to fixate on all the resumes you have out there and all the people who sounded like they were interested in hiring you next week, you're focusing on the wrong thing, and you risk losing focus.

Don't take it personally or get angry when you send out resumes and don't hear anything back. Most companies will not contact you to say they received your resume. You just have to assume that the fax machine you're using is working properly (for your reassurance, most fax machines display or print a message following transmission that states the number of pages that were sent successfully) and that your Internet Service Provider is doing its job, because employers don't bother with reassuring you that your fax or e-mail got through.

All you can do at this point is rinse and repeat. Get up the next morning and go to work looking for work. Just keep doing what it takes, until you get the phone ringing. If you utilize all of these suggestions, you should have plenty of resumes circulating, which increases your odds of getting called for an interview. Without an interview, you're suited up but still on the bench. To get off the bench and get in the game, you have to go on interviews. The best way to secure interviews is to do everything it takes to create a strong resume as discussed in the previous chapter and to get good at writing killer cover letters, which will be discussed in the next one. That, and put enough resumes out there that the numbers will work in your favor.

Set goals for yourself that state how many leads you want to come home with at the end of a day and how many resumes you want to submit each week. Learn your magic number. That's the number of resumes it takes before you get called for an interview (count only the number of resumes submitted to companies that actually have current openings when keeping track of your resume distribution). At the end of your first month of job searching, add up how many resumes you've distributed, and then count how many interviews you went on—if any. During the next month, double the number of resumes, and you should also find that you've doubled the number of interviews. Keep increasing the number of resumes you're distributing; the number of interviews should increase as well.

What happens if they don't increase? What should you do if you're getting twenty resumes a month into the hands of employers who currently have openings but you're not getting any calls for interviews? When that happens, it's time to look at what's on your resume.

IMPROVING YOUR RESUME

Some people with criminal records think they should wait until they get their record expunged, in cases where this is feasible, before they engage in a job search. They blame the lack of response they get after submitting resumes as proof that they need to clear up their record before doing anything else. Don't fall victim to this misguided line of thinking and use it as an excuse to procrastinate. The fact is, your resume doesn't even mention your conviction, so how could this honestly be the reason your phone hasn't been ringing?

If you're not having success despite your efforts, the real reason likely has more to do with either your cover letter or your resume. Make sure you have no grammatical errors, typos, or spelling mistakes on your cover letter or your resume, and that you're using the business letter format discussed in the chapter on writing cover letters. If you're not sure that you've constructed a resume without errors, have someone you can trust look it over.

If none of these elements is to blame, then the problem has to be about content. So, what can you do when your resume is holding you back? You have to improve it, which is simple enough to do. You need to follow these suggestions right away, though, so that time is on your side. This is what you need to do to improve your resume.

AGENCY WORK

When someone goes on vacation, when large projects come up, when people suddenly quit or get fired, or any other time a company is left short handed, they often call a temporary employment agency to help them fill the void. The temporary agency sends someone from their pool of people to work for the company for two days, two weeks, two months, or indefinitely. If the company likes the person, and if they seem competent and teachable, they're often asked to stay on permanently in one capacity or another. (Some companies even make it a practice to hire their permanent employees through temporary employment agencies. By bringing someone in on a temporary basis they can assess them before making them a permanent employee. Some agencies specialize in this kind of temporary-to-permanent, or "temp-to-perm," placement.)

Signing on with several temporary employment agencies can be one of the quickest and easiest ways for you to improve your resume. You will also benefit in several other ways by doing this. Here are ten benefits of signing on with them:

1. You add work experience and new skills to your resume, thus improving its strength.
2. You get your foot in the door, often with companies you would never get inside with a resume alone.
3. It is much easier to get a permanent position with a company once people have seen you in action.
4. You improve your appeal to employers—someone who is currently working is more appealing than someone who is out of work.
5. You add a current position to your work history and a current name to your list of references.
6. You earn money while you're looking for work, and, as your skills increase from one assignment to the next, so will your hourly rate.
7. You get to explore different kinds of companies and industries and expand the scope of your business knowledge.
8. You interview only one time with the agency, then go to several positions without the need to interview again.
9. The exposure helps you decide what kind of work you really want to do—this is a good way to explore opportunities.
10. When an employer asks you to tell a little about what you've been doing, you'll be able to mention your agency experience rather than less favorable alternatives.

So, what's involved in signing on with an agency? It's a pretty simple thing to do. The truth is, an agency needs to have a whole host of people to choose from, so they're hoping that everyone who walks through their door is someone they can use. They want to boast to companies about the number of workers at their disposal, so you're really playing in a different ballpark here. You submit a resume or fill out an application, they talk with you (sort of like an interview, but less formal) about your experience, and they promise to call you when they have an assignment that meets your skill set.

While you're in a different game, all of the business rules still apply—you need to sell yourself, so dress professionally and demonstrate the proper discipline, as if this was any other kind of job. They need to know you won't damage their reputation by being a bad employee—their reputation is on the line along with yours.

While many agencies generalize, others specialize in placing people who are skilled in certain trades or in the security, hospitality, accounting, legal, clerical, or medical fields. You will find them all listed in the yellow pages, or online, under "Employment Agencies, Temporary." Call the career center at the community college in your area and ask what agency is popular with the students. Agencies that specialize in work for students often have off-beat assignments that accommodate student schedules and their lack of work experience.

Try to find the best match by scrutinizing the ads and calling a few places. Unless you have a high skill set, you should tell them that you're looking for assignments in entry level positions and ask if they get those types of placements. Keep looking until you find a few places that seem like a good match for your skills. When you find one you like, sign on. Register with as many agencies as fit your skills, because if you don't have many skills, finding assignments for you will be more difficult. You will improve your odds of getting placed by signing on with several agencies.

VOLUNTEER WORK

Another way to improve your resume is by volunteering with nonprofit agencies. Nonprofits do community work with very small budgets, which means they are typically understaffed. Most of them couldn't do what they do without the help of volunteers. Consider what type of experience would most benefit you and your resume, and find an organization that would provide you with an opportunity to hone that skill. A good Web site to help you find a volunteer match is www.volunteermatch.org.

Once you find an organization you're interested in, place a call and have a conversation with the volunteer coordinator. Unfortunately, the volunteer coordinator is often a position itself held by a volunteer or a part-time person, which means they are not always available. You'll need to find out when that person is in the office and call back then. Don't wait to have your call returned, or you may end up waiting a while. Persistence is the keyword here.

When talking to the volunteer coordinator, find out what kind of opportunities exist. Tell them that you want to help out, but that you also want to increase your marketable skills. If you need office skills, then find a nonprofit that needs someone to do the kind of office work that's going to serve you best—stuffing envelopes, entering information into a database, filing, for example. If you want to increase your skills in construction, you would obviously want an organization like Habitat for Humanity that builds homes for low income individuals. Organizations that feed the homeless would be a good place to obtain food service or even janitorial experience.

By volunteering, your resume will be improved in two places: first, your Skills Summary section and, second, your Relevant Experience section. This should greatly increase the attention employers pay to your resume. If you have no work experience or very little work experience, list your volunteer experience on your resume in a section called "Community Service Experience." Place this section beneath the Work History section.

INTERNSHIPS

Internships are a third way to improve your resume and to gain experience. They provide short-term opportunities, usually in an unpaid (though some do pay very little) capacity and usually for students (though not necessarily), to gain experience in a field. Interns work in all sorts of companies, and the situation is win-win, for the company and the intern. The company doesn't have to pay someone for the work that gets done, and the intern gets to learn a skill and list new and valuable experience on their resume. You'll find internships on most job Web sites.

REFERENCES

The suggestions on improving your resume should be acted upon sooner rather than later so they can provide the best impact. Improving your resume while you're looking for work is one of the smartest ways to use your down time. By following these suggestions, you will also be helping yourself in one other very important area of the application process—references.

When employers feel they've found someone they're interested in, they tend to do a reference check. They will call your previous employers, and your current one unless you state otherwise, to see what they have to say about you. This recommendation will weigh heavily with the employer. How would you prefer to find a restaurant—by looking in the yellow pages, going there, and hoping for the best, or by going some place a friend has highly recommended to you? Of course you'd rather avoid the risk and go with the positive recommendation.

Well, employers are the same; they would rather hire someone that comes highly recommended over someone that was picked out of a pile of resumes and applications. After all, they know that resumes, just like yellow page ads, can often read better than the real thing is. So, to get a real sense of a person, employers like to talk to someone who has had first-hand experience with you.

When potential employers ask for a list of references, they're typically looking for the names of three people who know you in a professional capacity. If you don't have enough, or any, references right now, don't worry—you will after temping, volunteering, or interning to improve your resume.

So, make sure—if you're working in an unpaid position not to take the attitude that they're lucky to have you helping out for no pay. If you fail to respect the opportunity and demonstrate a poor work ethic you'll ruin your chance to have someone in a professional setting say positive things about your work. Be personable and work hard to make a good impression. It may be an unpaid position, but treat it with the same kind of respect you would if it was your dream job.

Remember, *don't* list as a reference the guy you have the most fun with. List someone in some level of management, and be sure to respectfully tell the person you've chosen that you've given their name out as a reference, and make sure it's okay. That way, they can expect the call and won't be caught off guard. If the person knows you by a nickname, tell them the name the employer will be using.

TALK IS CHEAP

If you've promised yourself that prison is no longer an option and that you'll do whatever it takes to get a job, then you now know what it takes to do just that. You know what an aggressive and concentrated job search designed to get you working quickly looks like. Take this information and run with it. Don't convince yourself that it's too much work. Remember, successful people are busy doing what unsuccessful people are busy complaining about doing.

Chapter 3

WRITING KILLER COVER LETTERS

Have you ever found a book at the library or a bookstore that had no cover on it? A book that just started on page one?

I doubt it. And if you did, it's even more doubtful that you borrowed it or bought it. The cover serves a certain purpose on a book, and it's ridiculous to think a reader isn't going to miss it.

Likewise, a cover letter serves a certain purpose for a resume; it's also ridiculous to think the employer isn't going to miss it.

Unlike writers of books, who never allow laziness or lack of skill to cause them to present a book without a cover, writers of resumes sometimes do— and they suffer the consequences as a result.

To send a resume to an employer without a cover letter is a waste of your time because the odds of your resume being read will be very slim. It doesn't matter how impressive your resume is, you're shooting yourself in the foot by violating this employment protocol. The natural conclusion that an employer would draw is that the person is either lazy or clueless. Would you want to hire someone who appears to be lazy or clueless? Some employers, in an effort to impress upon people its importance, have even taken to stating in their ads: "Resumes without a cover letter will not be considered."

How much more of a hint do you need? A cover letter *needs* to accompany every resume you send out.

The purpose of the cover letter is to present your resume, and yourself, to the employer—it's your first impression. It's your letter of introduction. It shows the employer that you gave some thought to the position you're applying for. It's your chance to outline the ways in which you're a good fit. It gives you the opportunity to highlight skills and talents that may not get across in your resume. It's also a good time to address potential red flags.

You can also use the cover letter to refer to work experience that may be too old or brief to appear in your resume's work history but experience, nevertheless, that would strengthen your qualifications for the position. The phrase, "though not reflected on my resume" is useful in these cases. For example,

> "Though not reflected on my resume, I am confident that the two years I spent in loss prevention would be put to good use in this position."

Think of your cover letter as being similar to a flashy news headline or a provocative book title—its job is to make someone want to read the next page. If the cover letter is written well, your resume will be picked up with enthusiasm. If your cover letter is a boring formulaic version of any other cover letter, your resume might as well be stuck in a brown paper bag.

The Internet age has increased the number of responses that employers get from their ads exponentially. Couple this fact with the fact that some positions, especially entry level positions, can draw large responses because of their few requirements, and you can only imagine the number of resumes an employer has to comb through. It makes sense, doesn't it, to make yourself stand out in the crowd when the crowd can be in the hundreds? The cover letter is the best way to make that happen since it's the first thing a potential employer sees.

When you finish this chapter, you will know how to write interesting, compelling cover letters that are unique and specific to the ad you're responding to—letters that will get the attention of potential employers.

THE NUTS AND BOLTS OF WRITING A COVER LETTER

So, what goes into a good cover letter? First of all, a good cover letter acknowledges exactly what the employer mentioned in their ad. Employers spend time and money to describe and advertise a position they're seeking to fill, and these details are what they hope to see addressed in a cover letter.

A customized cover letter shows you gave thought and attention to the needs of the employer as expressed in the ad. It makes a much better impression than a generic letter that reads as if it could be sent to anyone: "Here is my resume, I look forward to hearing from you." Unfortunately, it can be tempting to write only one generic cover letter that you use for all positions you apply to. This can be especially tempting if you don't trust your writing skills.

If you fear your writing skills will do you more harm than good, you will need to get help. If you're not sure when to use words like *they're*, *their*, or *there*, you need help. If you can't find the three mistakes in this sentence—"Its to late to find it's box."—you need help. Spell check would not flag an error in that sentence, because nothing was misspelled. But it's certainly poorly written and would look bad to an employer. (By the way, it should read, "It's too late to find its box.") No matter how wonderful a cover letter is, if it has grammatical errors, typos, or misspelled words, it just lost its value; this is a non-negotiable aspect of the cover letter. (You may find spell check and grammar check programs on computers to be useful, just don't rely on them.)

When writing a cover letter, your aim is to look at every descriptive word in the ad and see how you can address it in your own words or relate your work experience to it. This sentence deserves repeating, so here it is again: Your aim is to look at every descriptive word in the ad and see how you can address it in your own words or relate your work experience to it. For example, if an ad for a driver mentioned the person needed to be a good map reader, the employer is thinking, "We were very clear in the ad that we needed good map readers for this position. Therefore, if someone doesn't mention it in their cover letter, it must be because they don't have that skill."

Can you blame them for taking this line of reasoning? Don't forget that jobs don't always go to the better-qualified person but to the person who better pursues the position.

So, *your* cover letter, which of course tells the employer that you *are* a good map reader, moves directly to the front of those that don't, even if they might be better map readers than you are.

When describing your skills, you can say something like, "I am confident that my abilities in (name the skill) will be put to good use in this position;" or, "I have no doubt that my (name the skill) skills would serve this position well;" or, you can mix them. Sometimes you can even add in where and how you received your training. Here are some examples:

"I have no doubt that my map reading skills would be put to good use in this position."
"I am confident that the map reading skills I honed in the army will serve this position well."

Sometimes an employer will try to give you a sense of the atmosphere that you will be working in. They will make a point to state in the ad, for example, that "Applicants must be comfortable working in a hectic environment." Again, they wouldn't have mentioned that fact if that fact was not important, so acknowledge it in your cover letter. Using the framework described above you might say,

"I have no doubt that the extremely busy environment I grew accustomed to while working at Chucky Cheese would be put to good use in this position."

If necessary, use a thesaurus to find a synonym for the word used in the ad so you don't have to repeat the exact word (a synonym is a word that has the same meaning or nearly the same meaning as another word). If you looked up the word "hectic" in a thesaurus, you might find *frenetic* and *chaotic* listed as synonyms. If you're not familiar with the new words you've found, look them up in a dictionary to make sure you use the one that not only denotes the right meaning but connotes the right meaning as well. (After all, the song *I Left my Heart in San Francisco* just wouldn't have had the same ring to it if it had been titled *I Left my Pump of the Circulatory System in San Francisco*, now would it? That's the difference in denoting and connoting the right meanings.) The aim in doing this is to use active words that capture what the employer is looking for without restating exactly what they have said.

Let's say the ad stated that "this position is for someone who enjoys interacting with the public." You might want to mention in your cover letter that you're a *people person*, so that the reader will think, "Well if this person is a people person, they will enjoy interacting with the public." If the ad stated that the company was "looking for a reliable person to work the night shift," you might refer to yourself as *dependable* since that's another word for "reliable."

Sometimes ads have more than one descriptive word. If an ad said, "You will be required to turn in accurate weekly reports in a timely manner," what words would you address in your cover letter? If you said "accurate" and "timely"—good work. What do you do to make sure you turn in something that's accurate? You look for mistakes, right? One way to say that you're good at finding mistakes is to say you're "detail oriented," or that you "pay attention to detail." What do you do when you turn something in on time? You "meet deadlines." So, an appropriate sentence for your cover letter would state that you are

"a person who pays attention to detail while meeting deadlines."

An employer who reads that line in your cover letter will get excited about looking at your resume, and that's the idea. Remember, too, that cover letters can tell something that a resume would never state. As an example, what if an ad said "This position involves making deliveries to local bakeries and demands a 4 a.m. start." Ah, the perfect chance to state the fact that you're an early riser. If that was listed on your resume, it would be laughed at! But, in a cover letter, in response to this ad, it will be a tremendous plus. Let's look at an ad and an e-mailed cover letter that might respond to it.

Delivery driver. Looking for a reliable person to fill this driving position that starts at 4 a.m. Position entails making deliveries to bakeries in the tri-state area. Good map reading skills required.

Dear Hiring Manager:

While a 4 a.m. start would be a challenge to many, I have always been an early riser and would welcome a chance to benefit from that quirk in your delivery driver position.

I am also confident that the map reading skills I've honed over the years reading Thomas Guides would be put to good use, even though I am very familiar with the tri-state area. I'm equally confident that my dependability would serve this position well.

Below, please find my resume. I look forward to having an opportunity to speak with you on the matter.

Sincerely,

Pedro Gomez

The first thing a person reads in any letter is the introduction, so the introduction or introductory sentence needs to be an attention grabber in some way. While a boring, generic cover letter might start with, "Please accept the enclosed resume in application for the position of delivery driver," our introduction gets your attention right away by addressing a critical element of the ad—the 4 a.m. start time—with somewhat of a bold comment. It gets the letter off to a good start. The body of the letter should be used to address the skills mentioned in the ad in the way we've been discussing. To be clear and specific, it's important to list in the first paragraph the position you're applying for, exactly as it's stated in the ad. The closing should mention where the employer can find your resume.

"Please find my resume enclosed"
if the cover letter and resume are mailed

"Attached, please find my resume"
if the cover letter is e-mailed and the resume accompanies the e-mail as an attachment

"My resume follows"
if the cover letter and resume are faxed

"My resume follows, below"
if the cover letter is e-mailed and the resume follows in the body of the e-mail message

The key to writing killer cover letters is to take time with the ad and to let the employer's words sink in. You can't write a good cover letter if you don't take the time to really see what they're looking for. After all, your letter is basically a response to the following problem: "We need someone who can do this, that, and the other. Are you that person? Prove it." Don't start writing your cover letter until you're sure you can hear the questions they're asking. When you can hear those questions, you'll find your voice.

Here are some other valuable tips that will help you write killer cover letters:

Capture the impression the ad made on you.

Did it excite you to see the ad because you thought, "Wow, I'm a good match for this job; I can do this!"? If so, use that feeling to write your opening line:

It's rare to find an ad that seems to have your name written all over it, but that's how I felt the moment I saw your ad for a dog walker.

If I were to write a description of a position I would love to see myself in, it would be this one for an installer.

It's not often that you come across a position that feels like the perfect match, but that was certainly the case today when I saw your ad for a desk clerk.

It seems that jobs requiring respectable physical labor are becoming harder to find, but it looks like that's what you're offering and I know for a fact that's what I'm looking for.

Picture the position and the type of person needed to do the job right.

Reliable was the first word that came to mind when I read your ad for night watchman.
In the hospitality field, everyone who interacts with a guest is responsible for the
impression they make, and the maintenance staff is no exception.

Imagine the type of person that would not serve the position well given the details listed in the ad.

A company spends too much money in today's competitive marketplace attracting
customers to have them lost by ineffective employees.
I've always said that, if you're not a patient person, you won't last long in the
retail industry.

When you read the ad, did you immediately think back to something you'd done before?

Good memories came flooding back to me when I first read your ad for telemarketer.
For my first few years in customer service, I began each day with the mantra,
"Don't take anything personally."

Do you see how much more interesting these introductions are when compared to the generic "I am interested in the position of painter which you advertised recently in the *New York Times*."? A good introduction, or opening, is important to a good cover letter. But, sometimes it's helpful to write the body of the letter and then get back to the introduction.

Let's take the opening line from the last example above and finish writing a cover letter. Here's the entire ad:

Customer Service Reps
Bi-Lingual Spanish/English needed for check cashing
trans, money remit. Math skills, financial trans, etc.
PC Skills: MS Win 95, Internet $12-16/hr DOE.
Resumes: Jane Doe Fax (222)222-2222.

Remember, an ad is asking a question that your cover letter should be answering. This ad asks these questions: Can you speak Spanish and English?

Can you handle monetary transactions? Do you have math skills? Can you use a PC computer when the operating system on that computer is Microsoft Windows 95? Are you Internet savvy? Here's our response:

Dear Jane:

For my first few years in customer service, I began each day with the mantra, "Don't take anything personally." These words served me well then, and I'm sure they'll serve me well again in the position of customer service representative that you are seeking to fill.

Now that we have Jane's attention, we'll use our second paragraph to answer the questions she's asking:

I am confident that my bilingual skills, my competency with cash and numbers, and my computer literacy would be put to good use in this position.

Our final paragraph just wraps things up:

I welcome a chance to speak with you regarding this opportunity. Attached, please find my resume in application for this position.

Sincerely,

Sue Harrison

Since we didn't mention Internet skills, Jane is going to assume the answer to that question is, "No, Sue Harrison is not Internet savvy." But Jane is then going to think, based on information in the cover letter, "But that's okay because Sue is bi-lingual, which is much harder to find than someone who's Internet savvy. She says she's good with cash and numbers and she knows her way around a computer. Sounds good. Let's take a quick look at her resume."

Now, if Sue has read this book, she has added to her Skills Summary "Fluent in Spanish" to knock the ball the rest of the way out of the park. Is the power of the cover letter becoming clear now?

Sometimes an ad can be so short that it doesn't give you much to go on when writing your cover letter. If, for example, an ad just reads, "Janitor needed full-time. Fax 555-4267," you still need to make the most of the cover letter by capturing your skills concisely and showing how you would benefit the employer, just as if you were acknowledging a list of desires and elements in the ad. A response like,

"Whether it's waxing floors or scouring restrooms, maintaining grounds or cleaning indoors, I have the experience to perform janitorial tasks skillfully. And, as a self-starter, I don't require supervision to do so."

With only a couple of strong sentences, you've covered your experience and your ability to work well independently, which you know to be important in a janitorial position.

Think of words to positively describe your work experience, especially when this might help you explain a red flag on your resume. Don't just hope an employer will think the best about your resume if it's lacking something. Use the cover letter to address obvious negatives and shine a positive light on them. For example, if you've jumped around from company to company, which is a red flag to employers, refer to your work history as "diverse" or "multi-faceted." Say, for example,

"I am confident that the diverse work experience I bring to this position will serve your needs well. Whether it's the patience I learned while waiting on customers in the food service industry or the diplomacy I developed in my role as security guard, my multi-faceted background has prepared me for handling customers with courtesy at all times."

Never forget that your cover letter introduces your resume, so use it whenever possible to make that introduction a soft landing.

Hold on to all of the cover letters you write. Keep them on your hard drive or a portable disk of some kind if you can, but at the very least save a printed copy of each one. In time, you'll see that many of the jobs in similar fields have similar elements in their ads. You can save yourself from having to re-create cover letters by just making a few changes to one that you've already written.

If you hone this skill of writing killer cover letters, you will get the attention of the reader *and* stand out above your competition, every time— the same way a red sports car outshines a white sedan, every time.

KNOWLEDGE IS POWER

By paying attention to the terms and abbreviations used in ads, you'll grow familiar with the vocabulary that's appropriate for a given field, and you'll be able to use this language easily in your cover letters. (The same words will prove extremely useful in an interview, too, but more on that later.)

First of all, learn what your industry calls the people it serves. Some industries, for example, call the people they serve "customers" whereas others call them "clients," "guests," "passengers," "members," "alumni," "faculty," or "tenants." You don't expect your doctor to say to the nurse, "Who's our next customer?" any more than you would expect the guy at McDonald's to say, "Next client in line!"

You want to make sure you aren't making a similar mistake by using the wrong terms for your industry; and the more ads you read, the more informed you'll become.

You'll also need to be able to understand the abbreviations that are used in ads, both those that are used to save space (and therefore an employer's money) and those that are part of the industry you're interested in. You'll discover that common abbreviations can be found in the dictionary. If you looked up "trans," for example, from the ad above, you would find *transaction*, which explains what this ad was referring to when it said, "financial trans." "Money remit" is short for *money remittance* which might entail customers paying bills, or perhaps sending money overseas. When you see "DOE" written after an hourly rate, such as "$12-16/hr DOE," which appears in the ad, it stands for *depending on experience*. Based on that information, Sue knows that depending on her experience, she'll be offered a rate between $12 and $16 an hour.

Just like abbreviations, use the dictionary when you see other words you're not familiar with.

For example, if an ad said, "Looking for enterprising individuals for this co-op grocery store," would you just dismiss the ad because you didn't know what the words "enterprising" and "co-op" meant? Well, if you did, that might be unfortunate because you may have dismissed a job that was perfect for you: *enterprising* simply refers to someone who's full of energy and initiative and willing to take on new projects; a grocery store that's a *co-op* is one in which the employees also have an ownership role. This might actually be a great place to work, but if you didn't take the time to pick up a dictionary and educate yourself on those two words, you allowed those words to be a roadblock that they didn't have to be.

Knowledge is power, and sometimes that knowledge exists in something as small as the meaning of a word. Increase your power by gaining knowledge when reading ads. If you're reading ads online, you can find a simple dictionary at www.dictionary.com.

A thesaurus (also found at www.dictionary.com), as already mentioned, helps you find other ways to say something in your interviews and cover letters. For example, you could use "reviewed" instead of "looked over," "analyzed" instead of "read through." Learn to say you "facilitated" a support group rather than saying you "ran" it. You "merchandise" products when you arrange them on shelves in a specific order. You "assess" customer needs when you "figure out" their needs; you then "address" those needs when you do what they need to have done. You "organize" the supply room rather than "straighten it out." You are in charge of inventory, or in charge of inventory control or managing the inventory or controlling the inventory if you keep track of items that are on a shelf or who is taking items off the shelf or telling someone when it was time to order more items.

BUSINESS LETTER FORMAT

Don't take the time to compose an amazing cover letter and then damage its impact by failing to use a business letter format. This section will walk you through every step of what that format entails. Whether you're writing cover letters to be mailed or faxed, it is important to utilize the standard format for business letters. We'll start there, with printed cover letters, and then move on to cover letters that are being e-mailed.

Your letters first need to have a heading. To place your heading on a blank page, set your margins at 1" for the top, bottom, right, and left. To do this in Microsoft Word, click on the word "File" on the tool bar at the top of your screen and click on Page Setup from the drop-down menu. In the dialog box that appears, click on the "Margins" tab. Set the margins at 1" and click "OK." Your cursor will now be placed exactly where you need to begin, without spacing down to begin your heading. (*As mentioned earlier, if you don't feel comfortable using a computer, you may want to become a member of www.HelpAfterPrison.com to gain some computer literacy.*)

Once your margins are set, type your heading by filling in your name and contact information as in one of the examples below. Note that business letters do not use abbreviations in the heading. In other words, the words "South" and "Street" are spelled out, as is the state name. Two spaces should follow the state name before typing the ZIP code.

One other note about your contact information: Since a telephone call is still the most common way that a company will contact you, it is extremely important that the phone number you provide on your resume and cover letter will still be a working number two or three months down the road. (In addition, be careful not to have one number on your resume and another number on your cover letter.) No matter how amazing your resume is or how fantastic your cover letter, no one will put in the extra effort of trying to find a working number for you. Once the recording comes on stating, "The number you have reached has been disconnected," your chance at that interview is lost. If your living situation is temporary, give serious thought to the number you're going to use. Be sure to update your resumes if your number changes.

Example A

Marcus Johnson
P.O. Box 6543
Los Angeles, California 90003
213-755-4235

Example B

Marcus Johnson
P.O. Box 6543
Los Angeles, California 90003
213-755-4235

Did you see the difference? In Example A, the information is centered on the page while in Example B, the information is "flush left," or flat against the left margin. If you wish, for design purposes, you can draw a line under the block of information if you know how to; if you prefer not to make a line (or if you don't know how), that's fine, too.

Now, space down four lines (hit the return key four times) from the line or from the phone number if you don't have a line. Type the date. Spell out the date as shown in the example below; never use just numbers.

Space down another four lines from the date and put the company name (the place where you are applying) and the company address. If you know the name of the person you're addressing, put their name above the company's name, as shown in Figure 3.

Space down two more lines from that and write your salutation (your greeting, "Dear John"). If the ad doesn't give the name of the person you should be addressing your letter to, use "Dear Hiring Manager:" or, if you know the title of the manager it's going to, use that title—for example, "Dear Floor Manager:" or "Dear Day Shift Supervisor:" Also, notice that in business letter format you don't use a comma after the salutation, you use a colon. And, in case you didn't know, the days when it's okay to have no regard for gender and address a letter to "Dear Sir:" have long passed— don't do it!

Space down two more lines and start the first paragraph of the body of the letter. Do not indent your paragraphs; keep them flush left. If you have more than one paragraph, add an empty line between each one.

When you have finished with the body of your letter, space down two more lines and type your closing ("Sincerely"), followed by a comma.

Space down four lines from there and type your name. When you print the page, your signature will go in that space.

Your results should look something like the sample on the next page.

Figure 3

Marcus Johnson
P.O. Box 6543
Los Angeles, California 90003
213-755-4235

¶
¶
¶
¶
August 22, 2020
¶
¶
¶
¶
Cornelious Lockhart
Just Janitors
12334 South Main Street
Los Angeles, California 90001
¶
¶
Dear Mr. Lockhart:
¶
¶
Paragraph 1
¶
Paragraph 2
¶
Paragraph 3
¶
¶
Sincerely,
¶
¶
¶
¶
Marcus Johnson

By adhering strictly to this business letter format you will distinguish yourself as a professional.

FAXING AND MAILING COVER LETTERS AND RESUMES

If you're sending your letter and resume via fax, you need to fill out a fax cover page as neatly as possible so that your paperwork gets delivered to the right person.

In the rare instance that you're mailing a resume, you want to pay attention to your handwriting on the envelope. If your handwriting looks like an eight year old's, ask someone else to address the envelope for you or use the "print envelope" feature on your computer. Make sure the address falls in the center of the envelope, not at the top or in a corner. The left-hand corner should contain your complete return address in case the post office needs to return the mail. Do not write anything else on the envelope. Neatness and attention to detail will be noticed.

E-MAILING COVER LETTERS AND RESUMES

When sending a cover letter through e-mail (instead of by fax or mail), the format changes only slightly.

(1) Instead of putting your contact information in a header at the top of an e-mail, you put it at the bottom.
(2) You don't put the date or the company contact information. In fact, the company information will rarely be included if the company has requested that applicants respond by e-mail.
(3) Given differences (1) and (2), then, your e-mail actually starts with the salutation, such as "Dear Frank:"
(4) You don't leave four spaces for a signature since you can't sign an e-mail; you just type your name.

Here's an example of the letter used above with the few changes needed for e-mail:

Dear Mr. Lockhart:

¶

Paragraph 1

¶

Paragraph 2

¶

Paragraph 3

¶

Thank you for your consideration,

¶

Marcus Johnson

P.O. Box 6543

Los Angeles, California 90003

213-755-4235

One last *important* element about e-mail: make sure you turn off the "signature" feature on your e-mail that inserts "smiley faces," famous quotations, sayings, or other lines of text under your name—no matter how inspirational you think they are.

And another consideration: Be smart about the screen name you use when applying for jobs online. If your screen name is off-putting, insulting, or a take off on an obscenity, choose a more "boring" name for your job search purposes. An employer might think twice or three times before hiring someone whose e-mail was killer@yahoo.com!

If you don't have e-mail and would like to get a free account, you can go to either www.yahoo.com, www.aol.com, or www.mail.google.com. Follow the Web site's instructions to sign up for free e-mail, or "gmail," as Google calls it.

SENDING YOUR COVER LETTER AND RESUME VIA E-MAIL

You will often be sending your resume and cover letter via e-mail. This next section will explain step by step how to do that.

Until recently, the most common way to e-mail a cover letter and resume was to open a new e-mail, write your cover letter, attach your resume, and send it. Attaching a document is a very simple process.

(1) After writing your cover letter as the e-mail message, simply click on "Attach File" in your e-mail window. In some programs, this will open a dialog box where you can browse "My Documents," which are the documents on your hard drive. Or, from there you can click on "My Computer" if your documents are on a diskette of some kind. Clicking on "My Computer" allows you to see all of your drives, including the drive where you have inserted your removable disk.

(2) When you find the appropriate resume, click on the title or icon to highlight it, and then click "open" or "ok" or "attach."

(3) In a few moments, you will see the name of your document displayed in the appropriate spot of your e-mail as an attachment.

Today, though, many companies have become so wary of getting computer viruses by opening attachments that they are requesting applicants paste their resume into the body of the e-mail itself rather than attach it. Some companies even state that attachments will not be opened. In these cases, you will paste your resume below your cover letter in the e-mail. This is actually a good practice to use, unless you are requested otherwise, because you give the employer one less step to take (opening the attachment), they can immediately see what you have to offer, and they don't have to worry about system incompatibility (which can make it impossible for your attachment to be opened and read).

Pasting your resume into your e-mail is a little trickier just because you want to make sure the resume still looks "nice" after it's been sent. To begin, open the file where your resume is and copy the entire resume. Copy by highlighting the text—hold down the left mouse key while dragging the pointer on the screen to the bottom of the text, or hold down the shift key and use the arrow key to move the pointer down the page, or use some other method that you know. When the entire resume is highlighted, click the button on the right side of the mouse and select "copy." Now, close the resume document and put your pointer back at the bottom of the e-mail cover letter. Click the button on the right side of your mouse again and select "paste." Your resume should appear below your cover letter.

Next, e-mail the message to yourself. When you open it, you'll see that it probably needs some "fixing" to correct unintended shifts in the formatting. The primary problem you'll see are that the margins are a mess and some lines of text have been kicked down to another line so the ends of the lines are uneven. Clean up that problem by deleting extra paragraph markers that make new lines and extra spaces that have been created. Say, for example, two lines from your work history look like this:

Laborer   Mack & Sons Construction, Atlanta, GA   ¶
2005-2007
Stock Clerk   George's Grocers,   Savannah, GA   ¶
2000-2001

To correct this, put your cursor in a line and hit the delete key a few times and the space key a few times until the columns line up and the information gets back on the same line:

Laborer   Mack & Sons Construction, Atlanta, GA   2005-2007
Stock Clerk   George's Grocers, Savannah, GA   2000-2001

One other thing that doesn't tend to transfer well are any bullets that you may have used to list things, as used in Figure 2. They tend to transfer as bunches of symbols and numbers like ¢89938¢ rather than the • you expected. To correct this problem, delete the symbols and numbers and replace them with an asterisk. The asterisk sign appears on the top of the number "8" key and looks like this: *. To make it, hold down the shift key and hit the number 8, as if you were making a capital 8.

Make any other necessary adjustments and resend the message to yourself to make sure it looks okay. When it does, it's safe to send off to a company. A far more detailed way of "fixing" pasted documents involves converting the document into a text-only document first, making adjustments to it, then pasting it into your e-mail. If you're adept at using the computer, you can get step by step instructions on this process at www.susanireland.com

FINAL WORDS

You now know what goes into creating a cover letter that will serve as a great introduction to your resume and make you stand out from the crowd. You know how to find the key skills an employer has dangled in front of you in an advertisement. You know how a cover letter can be used to reframe red flags and to mention skills, talents, and experiences that may not be listed on your resume but could be selling points. And, you know how to package it all in a business letter format. In short, you now know how to write killer cover letters.

Chapter 4

MAKING CONTACT

While it's requested a lot less now due to the convenience of fax machines and e-mail, you may occasionally have times when your first contact with a company will be by phone. Some companies just continue to prefer this method of contact. If an ad tells you to respond by phone, you need to do so.

When calling in response to an ad, do so from a quiet place with no radio or television, no screaming kids, no crying babies—nothing in the background. Have the ad in front of you. When you're ready, take a few deep breaths and make the call.

If the person you need to speak with is not in and the receptionist asks if you'd like to leave a message, tell her that you're calling in response to the ad for whatever the position is and ask her when she thinks the person might be in. If she knows for sure when the person will be back, it might be better to call that person back at that time rather than set up a game of phone tag. That way, you won't miss each other's calls or be afraid to leave the house.

Call back a little later than the time you are told. If you miss the person again, you should leave your name and number.

Persistence is important, but there's no reason to leave repeated messages

again and again on someone's voice mail and certainly not with a receptionist in the same day. If you leave three messages on someone's voice
mail on Friday and you call on Monday and leave two more, by the time the
person gets in on Monday afternoon, they will have five messages from you
that say basically the same thing. You will appear more like a desperate
stalker than you will a persistent professional. It's okay to call frequently if
you have a direct number without a receptionist since you can then hang
up when the call goes to voice mail.

When you do leave a message, think about what callback number you are
going to leave. Although using a cell phone as a callback number prevents you
from missing calls, you risk having this very important call take place just
as the bank teller signals to you that you're next, or just as your phone's
reception drops out. So give serious thought to whether you want to leave
your cell phone as your contact number. If the cell phone is the only phone
you have and you get a phone call while in a loud environment or while conducting business of some kind, explain that this is your cell phone and ask if
the person can give you just "two seconds" to get to a quiet place.

CONNECTING

If a name is given in the ad, be sure to use it. If you live in a region of
the country where people tend to call strangers by a title and their last
name, follow that tradition; if first names are commonly used, take that
route. If the ad does not list a contact name, say something like,

"Hi, this is Pat James and I'm calling in response to your ad for a janitor.
Is there someone available I could speak with about that?"

With any luck, the receptionist will say something like this, revealing the
person's name:

"Sure, that would be Ryan. Hang on."

The next person coming on the line will be the person you want to talk to,
so be prepared.

"Hello. This is Ryan Jordan. Can I help you?"

You can then proceed to find out about the position.

"Yes. Hi, Ryan. This is Pat James, and I'm responding to your ad for a janitor; I was hoping you could tell me a little bit about the position."

The person will usually tell you a little about the position and ask you some questions about yourself. This miniature phone interview is your first chance to make a good impression, so don't sound dry and boring, like a detective just gathering facts. Sound interested in the position, and, if the position is appealing to you, sound enthusiastic about it as you gather information. *Your aim is to get an interview, not to learn everything about the job over the phone.*

Once the position has been described to you sufficiently, say enthusiastically, "Well that sounds great." Then ask, "What would be the next step in pursuing this position?" Ryan might then say, "Well, tell me a little bit about what you've been doing?" so you need to be prepared for that question. If you've followed the advice in this book and signed up with temporary agencies, you'll be able to answer with this perfectly fine answer: "Well, I've been doing temporary work, but I would like to get back into a janitorial position. I have more than three years experience as a janitor." Otherwise, you're in the position of hemming and hawing trying to find a way not to say, "I've been serving time in prison, and I'm looking for work."

If you're going to be asked to an interview, this is the moment it would happen. Make sure you know your schedule before you call about an ad; don't take up the person's time trying to remember if you're free on Friday at 2:00. Don't take their time asking for directions, either. If the location is difficult to find, the person you're talking to will undoubtedly offer directions. When you get the address, ask for a nearby cross street, but not for directions. You want to send the signal that you're a capable person, not to mention Internet savvy enough to get directions online. This is your first chance to send the message that you're competent, so take advantage of it.

End the call by enthusiastically confirming the time and day. "Great. Well, I look forward to meeting you on Thursday, Ryan, at 10:00." Then, get off the phone. Don't try to be funny, don't try to be witty—just get the information, make the impression, and get off the phone. You have accomplished your mission if you've landed an interview; don't blow it by going into your stand-up routine or asking unnecessary questions.

RECEIVING CALLS

Don't go through all the trouble of getting your phone to ring and then blow it by not being prepared when it does. Get ready for this phase of the job search. If you don't have an answering machine or voice mail, you *will* miss out on interviews while you're job hunting because there is only so much effort that will be put into trying to reach you. Answering machines are very inexpensive these days. In fact, you can find people either giving their old ones away or selling them cheaply as they get phones that have built-in machines.

Make sure your outgoing message on your answering machine isn't sending the wrong message to potential employers. You want to grab them at "hello" not send them running, and if your outgoing message is two minutes of your favorite music, you're really pushing your luck that someone is going to wait for the beep. If kids live in the house and answer the phone, make sure they know how to take messages.

If you're home and answer the phone yourself, your first impression has started at your greeting. In other words, if you've taken to answering the phone with any greeting other than a simple, "Hello," get back to basics until you find a job. If you're dodging bill collectors, child support people, or ex-spouses, you just might have to risk having a conversation you don't want to have because answering the phone and trying not to admit who you are until the person on the other end has admitted who they are sounds ridiculous. You only get one shot at a first impression, which is why it's called a first impression. When they call, they're trying to determine two things: first, do you sound like someone they should take the time to interview and, second, do you seem interested in the job. You're basically auditioning for the interview in this phone call, so make it good!

If there's noise in the room when the call comes in, excuse yourself to a more quiet room or shut off whatever needs shutting off. If you cannot immediately avoid or get away from the noise, it's better to ask the caller if they can hold on for a moment while you find a quiet place to talk. Try desperately to avoid beginning the conversation when the caller can still hear background noise, or worse, as you yell at someone across the room to be quiet or to turn off the TV. If you were running a business out of your home you would be professional enough to do this, so why not go about the business of your job search in an equally professional way?

When you do answer, remember that you have no idea who you're talking to or how much weight that person carries over who comes in for an interview. So, don't fool yourself into believing that the person calling to set up the interview is a nobody. This isn't the attitude that's going to get you employed. It's "game on" from the moment you answer the phone.

Be careful to use interview etiquette. Answer every question with a complete sentence. Don't say "uh-huh" instead of *yes*, or "uh-uh" instead of *no*. If the position the person is describing isn't ringing any bells, it's okay to ask for information to jog your memory; don't try to fake your way through the conversation. You're trying to make a good impression, and it will be harder to do that if you can't even remember the position they're talking about. Everyone knows that when you're looking for work, you're likely to be sending out lots of resumes, so they expect you might need a little information to distinguish them from other ads or to help you recall the position, especially if it's been a while since the ad ran. This is where having stayed organized will be helpful. If your job folder is handy, you should be able to pull out the ad and the resume you sent them so you are able to better present yourself, but do so only if you can do it without disrupting the call.

Make sure you keep a working pen and some paper near the phone. The key word here is *working* pen. Some people keep five or six pens near the phone, but when they need one—not one of them works. You don't want to keep the caller on hold as you try pen after pen—that gets old really quickly. What's worse is that some people don't even tell the caller they're still trying to get pen number three to work, and they allow the caller to continue giving information. The caller thinks you've been writing everything down when, suddenly, you repeat the first words they said as the last words you heard! "So, that was 155 . . ." You've just left the caller thinking, "Gee whiz, this guy is slow." What if you were expecting a call about some money you had just won and you knew they would need to give you an address of where to pick up your winnings. You would keep a pen that works and some paper nearby for that, wouldn't you? Odds are good that you would. Well, the call from an employer inviting you to an interview is the closest most of us will ever come to someone calling about getting some money, so it's a good idea to be prepared.

Get a phone number before hanging up in case you should need it.

If you weren't able to find the ad while you were on the call, find it as soon as the call is over and pull it out. You now have the name of the company and a phone number, two things you may not have had before, so attach this information to the ad, and take this page with you to the interview in case you need to refer to any of the information.

ARM YOURSELF WITH INFORMATION

Before your interview, get online and find a little information about the company. Find their Web site by doing a search with the company's name. (Do *not* ask for the company's Web site address while on the phone; you will look better by demonstrating your initiative to find it on your own.) When you find the site, read what's on the "About" page and what's in the press room or media room. This will usually provide the latest press releases or pieces of information about the company. You might even stumble across a news article that has been written up about the company, the competitors, or the industry.

What, exactly, are you looking for? Primarily, you want to know the mission of the company, which will help you get a sense of what's important to the organization. You might also want a sense of the company's size, the kinds of products and/or services it offers, and the number of locations it has. Once you've gathered all the information you can from the site, it's time to do a little snooping on the competition. To do this, simply do a new search using your city and state and the products or services the company offers, or you can go to www.yellowpages.com and do a category search there. Comparing the competition will help you explain to an interviewer why you are interested in them. Your answer can reflect that you know in what ways they stand apart from their competitors.

If the company is a "public" company (which means they sell stock), you'll be able to find additional information with your librarian's help.

The more information you find and learn, the better the impression you'll make when interviewing. Imagine the interviewer's thoughts when you say something that shows your knowledge about the company like, "Well, you obviously didn't get to be the fifth largest hotel chain in the nation without taking into consideration the impression your grounds make on an arriving guest. That's why I'm confident my attention to detail would be an asset in this position." In that one, single moment you came across as a professional who's on the ball. That means you're standing out in the crowd. It also may mean you just got the job!

Chapter 5

INTERVIEW LIKE
A PRO

Once you land an interview, you're officially off the bench and in the game. The interview is the next step in the job search. In fact, it's one of the most important steps—sitting in front of a total stranger, saying all the right things. There are no do-overs in an interview. There is no tiny speaker in your ear with someone on the other end feeding you your lines. It's only you and the experience you bring into the room—and your confidence. With so much at stake, it's difficult to understand why some people fail to practice.

Imagine a pitcher on a professional baseball team who's been on the bench all season. It's the bottom of the ninth inning in the play-offs. The score is tied, and the bases are loaded. Unfortunately, as the loaded bases prove, the pitcher has nothing left on his arm. The coach knows he needs to take the pitcher out because he needs to retire the next two batters without letting them get a hit. Now, imagine, if you can, the coach, with a trip to the World Series at stake, deciding to send in the pitcher who's been on the bench all year. Unless this is a Hollywood movie, you know the game isn't going to end well for this team.

Even when dealing with loads of talent, without recent practice, there's no guarantee of the outcome, and when you get only one shot at something with high stakes, the wise move is not to wing it. Your interview is typically your one-and-only shot at landing the position you're after, and if you go in winging it, without having practiced, you're not acting wisely.

So, prepare yourself for a little tough love: You *will* be bad at your first few interviews. No matter how many books you read on the subject, you will not be as good in the beginning as you will be after you've got a few interviews under your belt. Some things just require hands-on experience—swimming, working on cars, giving good interviews—in order to be good at them. Unfortunately, without experience, it's also difficult for you to tell what you need to practice; or even that you're bad at all! Unless you really bomb, you will probably think you did well.

For example, our first time out, most of us probably thought we were good drivers or good lovers, when in reality that's typically far from the truth. In time, with experience, we can look back on those early years and see how bad we really were because we then have something to compare it to. You'll think you're good at interviews, as well. You'll say good-bye to the interviewer, and he'll say, "Okay, thanks a lot for coming in. We'll be in touch." And you'll take that as confirmation that the interview went well. In time, you'll learn that this is just the polite way an interviewer ends an interview, and it doesn't necessarily mean a thing.

The more you practice interviewing, the better you will become. How do you get practice before you're actually *in* an interview? Well, you don't. Sure, you can set up a mock interview with a friend, but to get real practice you need to go on practice interviews. You need to go on interviews for positions you wouldn't want if they were offered to you. To find practice interviews, concentrate on ads that say "no experience necessary" or ads that say a position is "entry level" or especially those that say payment is based on "commission only." Such companies are often willing to interview anyone who shows enthusiasm. In addition, if a company pays on commission only, they're usually very liberal about who they hire since they need a sales staff and they're not taking a risk the way they would be if the position was salaried and they had to pay you regardless of your results. In fact, if you enjoy selling, this could be a quick way to get a job. The drawback is that the company doesn't pay you a dime until you sell something. But on the upside, since you're not a salaried employee, you typically have more freedom to create your own work schedule, which means that you can carve out job hunting time. Another way to find practice interviews is to look in the newspaper for companies that run the same ad week after week. This is usually an indication that for some reason or another the company does a lot of hiring. Fast food restaurants tend to do a lot of hiring as well. Wherever there's lots of hiring going on there's lots of interviewing going on, and that's where you want to be.

Don't set yourself up for regrets, get the practice you need. Practice may or may not make perfect, but it sure makes better. And, better is exactly what you want to be.

CONFIDENCE AND THE INTERVIEW

The more interviews you do, the more your confidence will build. In time, this confidence will be visible to the interviewer and you will be a more attractive candidate. Why is confidence attractive to an employer? Look at the definition of confidence: "Belief in one's own abilities." If interviewers can't see that *you* believe in yourself, it makes them doubt that *they* should believe in you either.

Say, for example, you've gone to a dentist for the first time, and when he walks into the room, he looks a little unsure of himself. When he shakes your hand, for example, it feels sweaty, just like the brow of his forehead. You quickly notice, too, that he barely looks you in the eye as he says, "My name is Dr. Scott." As he's explaining that he's going to take a panel of X-rays, his eyes dart around the room as if making eye contact would be painful. You ask him if he's having "one of those days," and he doesn't really respond. You make a little joke trying to put him at ease, and he doesn't smile. He leaves the room looking as ill at ease as he did when he first appeared. What would your opinion be of this guy? This could be the best dentist your city has to offer, but based on his actions, your gut is telling you this isn't the person you want working on your only set of teeth.

If, on the other hand, he looks you in the eye as soon as he enters the room, walks up and extends his hand, makes conversation and answers your questions—basically presenting himself as if he was the best dentist money could buy—you would have no reason to doubt his capabilities, and he would gain a new client. The only thing shaping your opinion in both cases is his confidence—or his lack of confidence.

Confidence attracts people to us and makes them feel better about trusting us or taking a chance on us. If you walk into an employer's office displaying no confidence in yourself, it doesn't matter that you're saying, "I can do the job," because everything else about you is screaming, "I *hope* I can do the job." *You have to correct this contradiction if you want to land a job.*

So, how do you go about building confidence?

The answer is you build it one experience at a time. You can't expect to be confident about interviewing if you have no experience or practice. We've all had times in our lives when we initially had little or no confidence in our ability to perform a certain act; but as we gained experience and practiced, our confidence soared. Gaining confidence in interviewing skills is no different. Your first time out might be nothing more than your introduction to the experience, so don't worry if your performance is unimpressive. This is why you want your first interview to be one where the stakes are low. The next time out, you'll have more experience and will feel more confident. You'll be familiar with sitting across from a stranger, being hit with one question after another. You won't be battling the fear of the unknown in addition to everything else, and you'll begin to find a comfort zone. As this comfort zone matures and expands, you'll continue to feel stronger in the interviews to come. When you know that you can deliver the goods, you'll come to expect it from yourself. This expectation exists because you've come to believe in your ability; and *that*, as you recall, is the definition of confidence.

THE "FIRST DATE"

So, let's look at the nuts and bolts of an interview. The interview is your first date, and you probably know what a first date feels like. No one wants to be on a date with a stick in the mud. We prefer someone who is enthusiastic; someone who is pleasant to be around; someone whose company we can enjoy and who seems to be enjoying our company, as well.

Interviewers want the same thing on their first date—they want to enjoy you. *People hire people they like before they hire people equally as qualified that they don't like;* never doubt this fact. Whatever traits you have that make people like you and make it easy for you to make friends—those are the traits you should let show during your interview. Be enthusiastic, smile, laugh at the jokes, don't be that stick in the mud no one wants to be on a date with.

Would you go out on a second date with someone who made you feel uncomfortable on the first one? Not if you're like most people. The interview is as much about your skills and abilities as it is about your personality. The truth is no one hires someone that makes them feel uncomfortable. People who are overly aggressive or overbearing, who look like they haven't smiled since the '50s, who can't look another person in the eye, who have body odor or bad breath tend to make people uncomfortable.

Interviewers are trying to find good workers as much as they are trying to find a good match for the community of workers they already have. If you make the interviewer feel uncomfortable, you won't get invited into the community—it's as simple as that. Think about it, when was the last time you met someone and said to yourself, "This guy makes me feel uncomfortable. I think I'll invite him home to meet my family"—it just doesn't happen!

DON'T MISS YOUR CHANCE

An interview is your chance to sell yourself *and* the interviewer's chance to sell the company and the position. Yes, there is mutual selling going on. But, the better a company, the less it has to sell you. And, the better your resume, the less you have to sell them. When people try to sell something, whether it's themselves or a used car, they tend to emphasize the good and de-emphasize the bad. That means that, while you're masking your weaknesses, the interviewer is shying away from the job's negative aspects. To make sure you're hearing everything you need to hear about a position, you need to be an active participant in the interview and not act as if it's a one-way street. You need to ask good questions to get the information the interviewer may prefer to hold back. So, don't just sit there answering questions like you're on a game show. If you do, you're likely to discover that you took a job with inconsistent hours, where you end up working forty hours one week and barely twenty the next, or some other equally unappealing quality.

To see if you've found a good match, you have to engage—sincerely engage—in the conversation while doing your best to absorb all the information being thrown your way. Not only is this the approach that will prevent you from accepting a job you really aren't suited for, but it's also an attractive demeanor to display in an interview. It demonstrates interest. What would you think about a first date who didn't ask you one single question about yourself throughout the entire evening? You'd probably think they weren't too interested in you. People want to hire folks who are interested in the job and in the company, people who are looking for a place to call their home away from home.

People who don't ask questions send the signal that they just want a job—any job. And that also sends the message that when a better job comes along, they'll want that job, too. You want to send the message that the position is important to you and that, if hired, you'll be there awhile. This is one of the reasons why you're highly encouraged to do your homework and learn as much about the company prior to the interview as you can.

If the interviewer has talked at the speed of light and has made it difficult for you to ask questions along the way, you should scribble down your questions as best you can, and, then, ask them when there's an opening in the conversation. The interviewer will likely offer you a chance to ask questions at the end of the interview, anyway. Although not as ideal, if left with no other opening, this is your opportunity to get your questions answered.

If, at some point, an interviewer says something that's unclear to you, interrupt them politely with a simple, "I'm not sure what that would look like" or, "I'm sorry, but I don't follow you." Those are nice ways of saying, "I don't understand," which is infinitely better than trying to fake your way through the interview hoping for the best. It also demonstrates to your potential employer that, rather than fake understanding when you're confused, you're going to ask good questions so you can do the job correctly.

THE "AHA!"

At some point in the interview, you'll have an "aha" moment. That's when you'll either realize the job doesn't sound like a good fit, or when you'll get excited and really want it. When this kind of excitement about the job hits, *be sure to let the interviewer see it.* You can be the best applicant on paper, but if you show no enthusiasm for the position, you can easily be passed over for the guy who was less impressive on paper but was excited about the opportunity to work for the company. It's just another one of the many social cues of our species: we expect enthusiasm to accompany desire.

So don't play Mr. or Ms. Hard-to-Get. Your eyes should say it. Your body language should say it. And, at some point, your mouth should say it out loud: "Wow, I have to say I'm getting pretty excited. This position is exactly what I'm looking for—I mean, exactly!"

When this kind of attitude comes after you've had the position explained to you, it reads as enthusiasm for the position. If you walk into the interview with this level of excitement, it comes across as creepy, so pace yourself.

FIELDING QUESTIONS

During the interview, you'll be answering many questions on many topics, but you must always remember that, no matter what single question you're answering at the moment, you're *really* answering the same ultimate question in several different ways: "Why should I hire you?"

When you're trying to sell yourself, you must use each question as an opportunity to give a little infomercial. Don't waste a single question by answering it with a "yes" or a "no."

We can all learn something, surprisingly enough, from the car salesperson when it comes to this. If you went to a car lot and a salesperson approached you and asked if he could answer any questions for you and you said, "Yeah, actually, I'm curious to know if this model comes with side airbags?" Would he simply give you a "yes" or a "no" answer? If you've ever been on a car lot, you know the answer to that is a definite no. A salesperson uses each question as a chance to either learn more about the customer or to sell them. His answer, then, might be something like, "No, they don't come standard, but I can get them installed for you." Or, "No, this model doesn't have that feature, but I have several other models that do." If the answer is "yes," it doesn't stand alone, either. "Yes it does. Is it important that your next car have side airbags?" There is no such thing as a "yes" or "no" answer when you're trying to sell something, whether it's a car or yourself.

Your answers should give interviewers a glimpse into your skills, your experience, your expertise, your talent, and your personality so they can see if you're the right person for the job and for the community you would be joining. No one is going to sit across from you and try to pull information from you. Some people think, "Well, he invited me for an interview so he must be interested in me. I'm sitting here so I obviously want the job." And then rather than showing that they would be a good person for the job they say things like, "If you give me a chance, you won't be disappointed." Or, "I'm willing to do whatever it takes to get this job." An interview is your chance to *show* that you won't disappoint them, to *show* that you have what it takes for the job. You may be a good match for a position, but if your answers fail to give the interviewer a chance to see this fact, you'll lose out.

Think about these opening scenes of a movie . . . A man is standing at the curb, trying to hail a cab, but no cabs stop; instead, they keep passing him by, but pick up pretty women only a few feet away. He continues with no luck. In the next scene, the camera is focusing on him in a cab, smiling. As the camera angle widens, you see seated beside him a very pretty woman. Now, imagine this instead: A man gets out of a cab, pays the driver, and turns to a pretty woman, who he's left in the back seat. "Thank you for sharing a cab with me since no one was stopping for me and I thought I'd have a better chance of getting one to stop if I stood beside a pretty woman like yourself who would agree to split the ride with me. Well, see ya." Which scene has a bigger impact? Clearly, the first story, which *showed* the action, was more effective than the second one, which *told* you what happened. In your interview, just like in a movie, you can either tell your story or you can have a greater impact by *showing* your story.

So, how do you show your story? The interviewer says, "Okay, John, as you know, we make chocolate here, and your job would be to package the chocolate in our one- and two-pound boxes. How does that sound to you?" You can *tell him,* "It sounds fine," or you can *show him* why it sounds fine: "That sounds great. I'm good with my hands, I enjoy repetitive tasks, and I'm sure I'd enjoy packaging chocolates." Now, that answer has some teeth!

You can make your answers even stronger by backing them up with past experience, by saying something like, "That sounds great. Several of my past jobs have involved repetitive motion in a fast-paced environment, and I really enjoy that kind of work. How many boxes per hour do most workers average?" Can you see how the person who answered, "Fine," doesn't stand a chance against either of the persons who gave the last two responses? *Telling* me you'll be fine is never as good as *showing* me with details, as in the last two responses. This last response also demonstrates the conversational style an interview should take of asking as well as answering questions.

Another good element to take from these examples is the way the candidates described the work as one involving "repetitive motion." This demonstrates that they were seeing themselves doing the work, which is exactly what the interviewer is hoping for. The last thing an employer wants to do is hire someone who hasn't thought through and really pictured the work involved only to have them quit two weeks after they start because they finally got the picture and they didn't like what they saw. This is why a good interviewer will do the job of painting the picture for you if it looks like you're not doing it yourself by saying something to the effect of, "Now, you realize that this involves standing on your feet for eight hours a day, right?"

If the position that has been described sounds difficult, dangerous, boring, exhausting, or anything that you would be better off realizing prior to taking the job, let the interviewer know that you grasp that fact. Asking a question before answering drives home the fact that you're really giving thought to the question and you're not just saying what you think they want to hear.

Consider this conversation:

Interviewer: Okay, John, as you know, we make chocolate here, and your job would be to package the chocolate in our one- and two-pound boxes. How does that sound to you?

John:	Would that involve standing in front of a conveyor belt the entire time?
Interviewer:	Well the chocolates do come down a conveyor belt, but you'll have a stool you can sit on so you won't have to stand all day.
John:	Oh, well that sounds very doable. This definitely sounds like something for me. I'm good with my hands, and my previous employers have always found me to be one of the fastest employees on the line.
Interviewer:	The job starts at 7 a.m. Is that going to be a problem?
John:	No, I've always been an early riser.

In his response to the first question, John asked a question of his own before answering. This shows that he's really trying to picture himself doing the work. Also, notice the last answer didn't stand alone as a "no" but rather a "no" with an explanation. In both of John's responses, he gave the interviewer a reason to believe him. An interviewer needs a reason to believe you, a way to be assured that you're not just blowing smoke, and explanations or examples or a mention of similar circumstances help them with that. Take a look at the next example:

Interviewer:	Rita, have you ever used a circular saw before?
Rita:	No, but I can learn.

Poor Rita. She just lost a few points with that answer. You always want to stay away from the "No, but I can learn" response. First of all, unless you have some mental or physical impediment, we can all learn, can't we? So you're really not impressing anyone with that information. Second, when you say, "I can learn," the employer actually hears, "You can teach me." What kind of a selling point is that? So, stay away from saying, "No, but I can learn" and instead think in terms of how your skills overlap from one job to the next.

Rita would have been much better off responding with something like, "No. I have to say the circular saw is one of the few saws I've never had reason to use. I've used a chain saw, a hack saw, and a jig saw, but the closest I've come to a circular saw would be a table saw, which I have several years of experience with. I've always thought of the circular saw as a table saw without the training wheels. After all my years handling a table saw without incident, I'm sure I'd have no problem taking the training wheels off."

Now *that* response gives us a good idea of what Rita is really capable of.

Get good at transferring your skills to current positions. Just because you're applying for a position as a dishwasher and you've never worked as a dishwasher doesn't mean that your previous jobs haven't prepared you to be a dishwasher. But it's up to you to show the interviewer how your experience or skill transfers to the job you're applying for. Here's an example of that:

Interviewer: Valarie, this position would require that you give ten-minute oil changes. Do you think you could handle that?

Valarie: Absolutely. When I worked in housekeeping at the Hyatt, I finished rooms in fifteen minutes—that included cleaning the toilet and the tub, making the bed, and straightening the room. Let me just say, if I can clean one room after another in fifteen minutes without losing momentum, changing oil in ten will be a snap!

Valarie has never changed oil before, but she has given thought to how the job she wants compares to a job she's had, and she does a good job of helping the interviewer see similarities that at first glance aren't easy to see.

One of the most important things you can do before the day of your interview is to think of all the ways the job you're applying for is similar to the work you've done in the past. Consider this justification, from Frankie:

"As you know, I don't have direct experience as a dog walker; I do, however, have several transferable skills that I think could be put to good use in this position. For example, when I was in child care, I developed a very watchful eye when taking the children for walks through the neighborhood. This is a skill I would now use when taking dogs for their walks. And, although I know some people find cleaning up after animals difficult, I can honestly say that won't be a problem for me given my janitorial experience where I cleaned up all kinds of messes."

After hearing Frankie's explanation, the interviewer is thinking, "Of course, how obvious. Of course this person can do this job."

That is what selling yourself in an interview is like.

You know in your heart of hearts when you can do a job even if your resume doesn't back you up. If you learn to speak in your cover letter and at your interview in terms of how your skills transfer, you will be able to break into new fields. If you get good at selling yourself, explaining how your skills transfer, showing with examples, and backing up your "yes" and "no" answers with details, you will convince your interviewer of what your heart already knows—that you should have that job.

INTERVIEW DRESS

Regardless of the job you're applying for, you must have appropriate interview clothes. Even if you're interviewing for a janitorial position or something in the trades, you cannot show up in jeans, a T-shirt, and sneakers. You can't dress like the person who already has the job; you have to dress like the person who wants the job. So, don't talk yourself into believing it's okay to show up to an interview in a pair of jeans because all the employees wear jeans to work.

An interview demands "dress attire," so do whatever it takes to legally acquire interview clothes. If you don't have access to buying clothes at a retail store, borrow clothes from a friend, find a used clothing store, or connect with an organization like www.careergear.org (for men) or www.dressforsuccess.org (for women) that provides free clothing to disadvantaged individuals entering the workforce.

Dress attire means a suit, a button-down collar shirt, a tie, and dress shoes if you're a man. Women may wear a pantsuit if that is accepted business attire for women in their region of the country; otherwise, a skirt or dress should be worn—the only consideration being that it's conservative— nothing that shows too much leg or too much top. If the position is a front office position or something where your wardrobe is important to the job, you really need to step up what you wear to the interview. Here are some additional pointers:

- Do-rags are unacceptable, as are hats or caps of any kind for men. If a woman wears a hat, it needs to be a fashionable outfit match.
- If your hair is scary, do something about it before you start going on interviews. If you wear your hair in a style that some people find objectionable, be prepared for this to impact your success in landing a job.
- Be sure to apply any perfume or cologne sparingly.
- Cover all tattoos and de-emphasize piercings by taking out any rings you may have on the face, and for men, this includes your ears. Once you're offered the job, you can ask how the company feels about tattoos or piercings being displayed, but you don't need to make things any harder than they have to be by displaying them at the initial interview. If you have tattoos on your face or neck, be prepared for this to impact your success in landing a job.
- Make sure your breath is fresh, but don't have anything in your mouth during the interview.
- Do not wear sunglasses or have them resting on your head.

INTERVIEW ETIQUETTE

Make sure to bring a pen to the interview, not a pencil. A pencil isn't what a professional uses in an office setting to take notes during a business meeting. If you need to fill out any forms or paperwork, a pencil will be unacceptable, so bring a pen and project the right impression. (And, make sure the pen writes before you leave home with it.) In addition, take a note pad of some kind. If you can't afford one, simply get a manila folder that some stationary stores sell individually for about a quarter and put some paper inside of it for taking notes. (Stay away from the kind of spiral bound notebooks kids use for school.) That way, you can take very brief notes during the interview about the position and the company (just don't go into court reporter mode). And, as stated earlier, you might find it helpful to jot down questions as they crop up if you can't ask them right away.

Turn your cell phone *off* before you enter the building; the last thing you want is to have your phone ringing or vibrating in your purse or pocket in the middle of an interview. Yes, even phones that are set to silently vibrate tend to still make a sound that can be distracting, so turn them off. Likewise, from the time you enter the building until you leave it, don't pull out any devices for music or games. (In addition, do not take friends or your husband or wife or kids along with you; if they have to come, make sure they don't enter the building.)

When shaking hands, make sure you use a firm grip. (A "limp fish" hand-shake feels horrible, and "the preacher's handshake"—cupping the left hand over the right—is just plain weird coming from a stranger. Neither of these handshakes makes a good first impression.) While shaking hands, smile and make eye contact. You've probably heard a million times the importance of maintaining good eye contact in an interview, but the handshake moment may be one of the most important moments to remember that point. So much of what we conclude about a person is drawn from the initial few seconds of meeting them, and someone who can't look you in the eyes and smile while shaking hands is sending a negative message.

After shaking hands, the interviewer will most likely offer you a seat. If so, respond with a "Thank you." When you sit, use the correct posture, and demonstrate a demeanor appropriate to an important business meeting: feet flat on the floor, body alert and responsive, no slouching, the small of your back resting against the back of the chair.

Be aware of your mannerisms: Don't twist your hair, rub your chin, stroke your beard, or play with anything else on your face when you talk. Don't sit in a chair like a pimp rides in his car, leaning to one side. Don't lean forward on your elbows. These are mannerisms you need to make note of and avoid.

Don't use slang or street language. Neither has any place in an inter-view, regardless of how common an expression or how "down" the person interviewing you looks, even if you think they share your background. Avoid phrases like, "Ya feel me?" or "See what I'm sayin'?" And, *don't* pepper your answers with "Ya know, . . ." or the word "like—"

Speaking of language, there is no such word as "hisself." Look it up; it doesn't exist. So, if you're saying, "He did it hisself" when you should be say-ing, "He did it himself," you're not speaking English. Two other unforgivable mistakes are "I seen . . ." and "I done . . ." Think back to grammar school English class. I s*ee* him. I *saw* him. I *have seen* him. I *do* it. I *did* it. I *have done* it. This means every time you say, "he done it" or "I seen it," someone is cringing—don't let it be your interviewer.

On the other side of the coin, do not try to impress the interviewer by using large words. Too frequently, the person who tries to impress people with their vocabulary will tend to use the *wrong* large word. It's better to use a small word correctly than a large one incorrectly. There's no shame in using small words that effectively make your point; no one will judge you poorly for it, but it's easy to lose your credibility when you use a large word incorrectly.

If you don't have any activities in your life that demand professional language on a regular basis, it's easy to end up talking as if you're speaking with friends. That's yet another reason why practicing your interview can be so important.

WHAT TO EXPECT

Usually, an interviewer will engage in a little small talk prior to launching into things. This warm-up is meant to relax you and to build a little rapport. Don't miss the opportunity to connect with your interviewer at this stage of the interview. Chuckle at whatever joke is made, and even add to it if you can. If the interviewer thinks the weather has been horrible this week, so do you. This is your first chance to show your personality, so connect with the interviewer and provide them a glimpse of yourself. The warm-up is usually very brief, anywhere from 15 seconds to a minute, but take your cue from the interviewer as to when it's over. The interviewer is the talk show host and you're the sidekick—that means they're leading the show and you're following their lead, no more, no less. When it looks like they're ready to get down to business, be the good sidekick and follow suit.

In the next phase of the interview, some interviewers will describe the position and the company first, to let you get a good sense of the position you're there to discuss. They will then ask you some basic, general questions about yourself and your experience, perhaps while looking over your resume.

Other interviewers will start off with an effort to get to know you first. They often do this by going over your resume with you and having you tell them a little about yourself and the companies you've worked for. They may then transition into asking about your interest in their position. This will then be followed by the interviewer describing the company and the position.

There are some standard questions most interviews include. Prepare yourself by rehearsing the answers to these questions so you don't feel and look like a deer caught in the headlights. The most common question, and often one of the first, is, "Tell me a little about yourself." Now, that's obviously a simple question, but the answer is anything but obvious.

"Tell me a little about yourself."

First off, you don't want to answer this question for your interviewer, who is looking to see if they want to hire you, in the same way you'd answer someone you've met at a club. If I'm your interviewer, for example, I really don't care what your favorite blog is, or that you used to be in a band, or that you play basketball on weekends. I want to know about you *only as it pertains to the work environment*.

Second, don't let this question lull you into revealing things that are illegal for the interviewer to ask in a straightforward manner or into revealing information that might be used to discriminate against you. For example, don't talk about being a proud parent of three beautiful girls, or being your son's little league coach. People prefer to hire folks who have no children because children tend to get sick unpredictably, which can affect an employee's attendance; but, it's illegal for them to ask if you have children. Don't reveal any religious or anti-religious aspects of your life—interviewers cannot legally ask those types of questions, either. And, although your recovery program may be one of the biggest aspects of your life and you're proud of it, revealing a history of addiction unnecessarily may give your interviewer pause to reconsider your eligibility. Even something as positive as going to school in the evenings to get your degree may send up a red flag to an employer—*How will this extra activity affect this candidate's performance?* Or, it might cause him/her to become suspicious that the job is a short-term gig—*And what happens when this candidate finishes school?* (An exception to this is if you're pursuing a degree in the field you're applying for so that you'll be stronger in the position.)

So, what is an appropriate answer to the question? Carefully, use this question to offer information that benefits you. For example, explain why the field interests you, mention things that make you sound stable.

"I've been interested in facilities maintenance since I can remember. Maybe it's because I like things orderly, but I do find it to be a good personality fit. I'm the type of person who enjoys a job where you can immediately see the results of your work. I have deep roots in the community—I was born and raised here, and I plan on retiring here. I'm looking for a company I can grow with; the last company I was with couldn't keep pace with the industry and had to eventually close. I don't want a repeat of that, so I'm focused on finding a company that has a track record. That's what brings me here today."

Notice that this response paints a picture of the individual behind the resume *and* contains useful, appropriate information for the interviewer. It tells a short little story that wraps back around to the matter at hand. It also mentions things that are positive to the ears of an interviewer and therefore benefits you.

We all have plans for our futures that change along the way. To share information of this kind and miss out on a job for something that may or may not come to pass is unwise. The fact that you see yourself moving out of state in a couple of years, is not beneficial, so it's not something to be mentioned. If your plans are to join your cousin's moving business but you need a job until he can afford to bring you on board, you have absolutely no reason for sharing the information with an interviewer—after all, you really have no idea when or if this idea will ever come to pass. But, no one wants to hire someone who sounds like they're just passing through.

"Why do you want to work here?"

Another very basic and common question is actually a set of questions: "Why do you want to work here?" and "What made you choose us?" The importance of answering this question thoughtfully can easily be seen by imagining asking a date, "So what made you agree to go out with me?" and hearing the answer, "Well, to be honest, I didn't have any better offers at the time, so I said, 'Yes!'" If you're not thoughtful when answering the question, "Why do you want to work here?" you risk giving the equivalent of this bad answer. "Because you were hiring" or "Because I need a job" or "Because my friend works here and told me you were hiring" are answers that are as improper as your date's response.

What you want to hear from your date is something that makes you feel good about yourself, something that implies there were plenty of other people your date could have chosen but you were the pick because . . . . *That's* the kind of answer you're wanting from your date and *that's* the kind of answer your interviewer is expecting from you.

A good way to answer the question is to use what you know about the company and tie it into your career goals. This is a time when the research you've done on the company will come in handy, even if all you did was visit their Web site.

"I'm interested in pursuing a career in the grocery industry, and, when I learned that your grocery was a co-op, it sounded like the place for me. I like the idea of not just having a job, but actually having a stake in the company."

Did you learn the size of the company from the Web site?

"I want to work here because I want a job in the transportation industry, and, if it's possible to drive for a company with the kind of reputation you have—being the fastest growing courier in Baltimore—then that's where I want to be."

Did you research the competition?

"I'd like to work here as opposed to other companies in the industry because no one else comes close to the customer satisfaction rating you have. I take that as an indication that you probably have a happy staff of employees, as well."

If the company is well known, that's information you can tie into your answer, too.

"I love driving for a living, and I've always imagined working for a company that was a household name. When I saw your ad, I got excited. Because you've been in the public eye for so long, I feel like I already have a sense of the way it would feel to work here, the way you want customers to be treated, and the expectations you have of your employees. It feels like a good match for me."

The reverse of name recognition is the Mom-and-Pop operation.

"I want to work here because I enjoy the spirit of a small company. It doesn't appeal to me to be Employee Number 1531 at a large corporation. I'm the type of person who really gives their all, and I think that can be under-appreciated in large companies. That's the lifeblood of an operation your size, though, so when I saw your ad, I had a good feeling about it. And I really appreciate this opportunity to talk to you about what you're looking for."

"What experience best prepares you for this job?"

Here's another question you want to give a lot of thought: "What experience best prepares you for this job?" Only *you* know the answer to this question. And you want to make sure that your interviewer knows as well, since it's at the core of what they're asking themselves as they scan your resume. You want to respond to this question so readily and with such a high level of enthusiasm that the interviewer is blown away by how much thought you've given to this question. If possible, use your answer to drive home a point, or points, the interviewer has made. If, for example, when describing the company to you, the interviewer has made a point of trying to convey how extremely fast-paced the environment is or how demanding the customers can be or how the position entails very physical work, tie these warnings together.

"Well, I asked myself that question before submitting my resume. When you were describing earlier how hectic it can get around here during lunch, it reminded me of my days as a messenger. The reason I did so well there was because of my ability to keep several plates spinning at once without letting any of them drop. I have a strong feeling I'd be drawing from that skill in this position."

"Where do you see yourself in five years?"

Another common question, but one that can catch you off guard if you haven't given prior thought to it is, "Where do you see yourself in five years?" Again, you only want to disclose information that benefits you. If your first inclination is to mention that you would like to be living in another country five years from now, ignore the urge to share. Remember, this question isn't the time to disclose all of your wish-upon-a-star ideas, and your answer should pertain to the position. If you see your band getting off the ground in five years, keep it to yourself; the same is true for starting your own business, going back to school full-time, or starting a family, especially if you're a woman. Though today's companies realize retaining an employee for more than two to three years, especially in entry level positions, is a lot to hope for, when you say it out loud, it's just bad form. Your answer to the question should center on career goals, in keeping with the job you're seeking at that moment.

"Well, to be perfectly honest I would really like to be in management in five years or less. I've always been told I have good people skills, and I tend to end up as the default leader in most situations. Given that I'm good at what I do, five years from now, I would expect that I'll be even better at what I do and in a position to help others learn from my experience."

If you're breaking into the field and have little or no experience, you may want to briefly state something like, "In five years, I see myself with a foothold in this industry." This response sends the message that you're not just here because the position doesn't require experience; you're here because you want to carve out a career in the field, and your long-term plans involve staying in the industry.

"Why did you leave your last job?"

Interviewers can learn something about your character by the way you respond to this question. First off, you need to answer honestly. A simple reference check will reveal that you were not "laid off," as you claimed, but rather that you were fired.

On the other hand, don't be *too* honest. Don't, for example, bad mouth your former boss or the company. Doing so can lead interviewers to suspect you might do the same when it's their company you're talking about. So, even if you quit a job because you worked for the biggest idiot in the industry and even if anyone who met the guy would agree, to describe the situation in such terms is bad form in an interview.

Yes, honesty is important when answering the question, but it needs to be tempered with diplomacy. Going into details about supervisors showing favoritism or racism or disrespecting you is not the approach to take here. The approach to take with this question is to avoid telling the story behind what led up to your leaving and instead summarize the reason for leaving down to a few concise sentences that end with a positive spin.

If you left your last job because you were fired, or you were arrested, you want to give careful thought to the most honest way of answering the question while keeping it simple, brief, and forward-looking.

"Although circumstances caused me to leave that job, it was a learning experience that I would put to good use in this new opportunity."

"My boss and I agreed that my skills weren't a good match for his needs at that time, and I'm happy to have moved on."

"Unfortunately, I allowed certain personal problems, which have long since been resolved, to prevent me from bringing the best I had to offer to that position and it naturally led to my pre-mature release. But more importantly, as I said, those set of circumstances have found resolution."

These are very standard questions you can expect to be asked in most interviews. Preparing for them in advance will go far in setting you at ease and improving your self-confidence.

CAR Questions: "Describe a specific situation when you . . ."

Another type of question you should prepare to answer is more complex than those covered so far. Interviewers love to have applicants describe a situation in which they had to use a particular skill listed on their resume. Interviewers love these questions because they accomplish several things at once:

1. They see if you do, in fact, possess the skills you have listed on your resume.
2. They see if you can communicate effectively.
3. They see if you can think on your feet by answering a more complex question.

You should love this type of question too, because if it's asked, you know it's also being asked to your competition, and, they're probably blowing it by telling an unprepared and disjointed, but perhaps entertaining story. You, on the other hand, will follow the CAR (Challenge-Action-Result) structure to answer this type of question, which is exactly what an interviewer wants.

Let's look at a possible CAR question. Say, for example, your resume lists the fact that you have customer service skills. A question you might, then, be asked is, "Describe a specific situation when you provided excellent customer service in your most recent position, and explain why it was effective?"

This is how you answer this question using CAR: the *challenge* is the situation you found yourself in; the *action* is what you did to handle the situation; and the *result* is how the situation ended.

You should know that CAR questions often have lengthy answers, so take time to paint a complete picture. Here's one possible answer to your question:

"One time, I had a customer who was upset when he got to the video store and found out that we hadn't held a movie we promised to hold for him until 6:00. It was only 5:30 when he got to the store, and it appeared that the last copy had just been rented by another customer. He was pretty upset after driving over just for that one movie, and he told us that the only reason he still came to our small store rather than going to the larger outlets was because of the service we provided. If we couldn't get that right, he said, he saw no reason to keep using us."

That was the challenge. Here comes the action that demonstrated excellent customer service.

"While apologizing, I got on the computer and discovered that, while the movie wasn't on the shelf, it should have still been in the store, which meant that one of the other three customers in the store at the time probably had it in their hands. I excused myself and took a quick walk around the store, found the gentleman who had it, and explained the situation. He agreed to let me have the movie. In return, I offered to give him his rental at no charge."

All that's left now is the R, the result:

"Being able to think on my feet saved us a customer. I'll never forget the look on his face when I walked up with the video in my hand, apologized again, and then told him the rental was on the house for the aggravation and confusion. His stock in our little store went from zero to off the chart in that single moment because of the customer service I provided him."

Train yourself to think CAR whenever your interviewer begins a question with "Describe a specific situation when . . . ." By using this structure to answer this more complex question you'll be able to construct a strong response and impress your interviewer in the process.

QUESTIONS, QUESTIONS, QUESTIONS . . .

Take time before your interview to consider and plan how you would answer all of the types of questions discussed in this section. By preparing in this way you should be ready for any variations they may throw your way. If you prepare and practice answers to each of these questions and also think of how you would answer a CAR question about each of the skills you listed on your resume, you shouldn't have any surprises when it comes to fielding interview questions. Here are the questions again:

"Tell me a little about yourself."
"Why do you want to work here? What made you choose us?"
"Where do you see yourself in five years?"
"What experience best prepares you for this job?"
"Why did you leave your last job?"
"Describe a specific situation when you . . . "

Other questions you might want to give thought to include:

"What did you like most about your last job?"
"What are your greatest strengths?"
"What are your weaknesses?"
"Why do you feel you are the right person for this job?"

Make sure you listen carefully to the question being asked, and don't assume you know what's coming. Wait until the interviewer completely finishes talking before answering; interrupting is a definite no-no. In fact, take a moment to absorb the question (and take a long breath) before speaking; the interviewer is expecting thoughtful answers, so there's nothing wrong with taking a few seconds to form those thoughts.

One final point on answering questions can't be stressed enough. Always, always, always think about the message your answers send to the interviewer. Don't create roadblocks for yourself by answering questions without giving thought to that message.

For example, if you're asked, "Why did you leave your last position?" don't answer, "Because it was boring." If you do, the interviewer is likely to ask you something like, "So, you left your last job because it was boring, but this position involves boxing chocolates all day long—what's going to prevent *this* job from getting boring in a couple of months?" And there you are—without even realizing it, you've just painted yourself into a corner because you didn't think about the message your answer would send.

Chapter 6

HANDLING THE BIG QUESTION

You must be 100 percent prepared to answer the million dollar question. It will likely appear on a job application as a variation of "HAVE YOU EVER BEEN CONVICTED OF A FELONY?"

Let's be clear about handling it on the application if you have to fill one out. First, be sure to read *carefully* what the question is asking: felonies versus misdemeanors, convictions versus arrests, and convictions within the last seven years—all mean different answers. Don't offer more information than the question is asking by failing to read it carefully. But at the same time, you must be honest when answering.

Yes, some people do choose to lie and then hope for the best. The risk you take when you lie is summed up in the fine print of the employment application, usually right above the signature line. If you take the time to read it, you'll see that it basically says "your signature certifies that all the information you've provided is true to the best of your knowledge and that any misrepresentation or false statements are grounds for dismissal." People who have chosen to roll the dice with their careers tend to lose the roll.

They may be hired initially and think they've gotten away with lying because they were hired, but companies are sometimes just slow in getting background checks done or in looking over the results when they come back. Once they get done, though—and background checks are so easy and inexpensive to run these days that the majority of companies will run them—the person will be immediately fired because they lied about the felony. Sometimes, a lie will not be caught until new management takes the helm and makes their first action a sweeping round of background checks; sometimes, a promotion includes a new background check. Suffice to say, if you lie, you can never rest easy that you have a job for the long-term. It's far better to be secure and at peace in the fact that you have honestly acquired the job than it is to roll the dice and hope for the best. Let's face it, if you've served time, you've already been caught doing something you expected to get away with—living proof that it's not always as easy to get away with something as you might think!

The better and wiser alternative to gambling with your career is to answer the question honestly. On an application, beneath where you answer "Yes," you'll usually find a space provided for explanation. Write in "Will discuss during interview." That's better than trying to supply details on the application.

If, instead of filling out an application, you've submitted a resume, a gap in your work history will probably be the cue that triggers the red flag. In that case, you'll already be in the interview, so let's get into a discussion of answering the big question.

THE EMPLOYER'S PERSPECTIVE

So, how do you then discuss the question in the interview when it's brought up? Well, that is certainly *not* the time to wing an answer. It's very important to take the time in advance to evaluate your conviction in terms of how you can describe it to an employer in the best light possible. How much or how little you should say hinges on the specifics of your offense. To help you determine the answer to this question, it might be helpful to look at it from the standpoint of the employer because there are a few elements an employer considers when weighing the decision to hire someone with a criminal record or not.

An employer is more likely to hire someone with a criminal record if

- the offense did not happen recently
- the offense was a non-violent offense, such as drug possession, and you have remained drug-free since
- you have utilized the services of an intermediary agency like the organizations designed to help previously incarcerated individuals with job readiness and job placement
- you can show that you are improving your life
- you have had meaningful work experience since your release

THE PSYCHOLOGY OF WORDS

Now let's look at answering the big question using the best language possible to describe your offense. No matter how you describe your offense, start the explanation with something to the effect of, "I'm glad you asked because I want you to feel comfortable about hiring me." Another opening line, if the interviewer asks about the gap in your work history, is to start out, "To be perfectly honest, during that time I was paying a debt to society for a mistake I made."

From either beginning, continue by using the psychology of words to your advantage as you paint an image of time. For example, it's true that a decade is the same as ten years, but doesn't "a decade" sound like a longer period of time than "ten years?" Isn't it also true that five years ago is "half a decade" ago, and six years or more is "almost a decade" ago? Yes, it's true. So, use these words to your advantage and paint a picture of a *distant* past. Remember, too, that unlike on the application, in the interview you're talking about the time that has passed since *the act itself took place*—not the arrest, not the trial or sentencing, and certainly not the length of time since your release. . . you're counting time from the time of the act itself.

One other important note here: Refer to your conviction as "a mistake." We don't all have convictions in our past, but we do all have mistakes in our past. Your aim (as we've discussed before) is to find common ground with your interviewer. Unlike the word *conviction*, the word *mistake* conjures an image everyone can relate to, and that equates to a common ground.

FRAMING YOUR RESPONSE

Now that you have this knowledge, you need to sit down and craft your answer to the question. It's true, you only have to work with what you truthfully have to work with, but, regardless of the nature of your offense, your presentation of the situation and the language you use to describe it are crucial. Here are some examples of wording that should be helpful in framing your description:

"It was an isolated incident."
"It was an unfortunate time in my life that's behind me now."
"It was a misdirected time in my youth."
"That young person doesn't even resemble the person I am today."
"That regrettable time in my life is very far removed from the clean and sober person I am today."
"My crime involved no victims except for myself."

Let's look at each of these separately:

"It was an isolated incident."

Was your crime a first offense? If so, it sounds better to describe it as an "isolated incident." The use of the word "first" makes people assume there was a second or third. You don't typically talk about your first wife, for example, unless you've had a second wife. So, although *you* understand the meaning of the term "first offense" others may think you mean the first of multiple offenses, which makes it a poor choice of words. The definition of *isolated*, on the other hand, is "not occurring or happening regularly." And, that's exactly the image you want to create if this is the case.

"It was an unfortunate time in my life that's behind me now."

If your crime was not isolated and you have several convictions on your rap sheet this is one way to describe it.

"It was a misdirected time in my youth."

This construction provides the all important distance employers appreciate while, at the same time, emphasizing that the crime probably had something to do with the stupid things we all call "good ideas" when we're young. Many of us regret some of the choices we made as young people and realize that the actions of our youth don't always accurately reflect the people we are today. This language encourages an employer to think in these terms.

"That young person doesn't even resemble the person I am today."

This description paints a similar picture as the previous statement. It simultaneously creates distance while advancing the idea that it makes no sense to fear the person you are today because of the exploits of your youth.

"That regrettable time in my life is very far removed from the clean and sober person I am today."

As previously stated, if your offense involved drugs, employers want to feel confident that you have been clean and sober since that offense. This description paints that picture.

"My crime involved no victims except for myself."

In some rare cases there are no actual "victims" associated with a conviction. By framing your conviction with this wording, you're letting the interviewer know that although you *have* committed a crime you didn't *victimize* anyone. This information may help to calm the fear of many employers that you'll victimize again, and, this time, it might be the company, employees, or customers.

WHEN TO SAY MORE OR LESS

As you continue to explore the best language for explaining your conviction, it's important to look at your offense through the eyes of the employer. Now that you know the elements an employer considers before hiring someone with a record, use this information to your advantage.

Violent Offense

Clearly, it would be better if your offense was non-violent, but if it was violent, there's no way to change that fact. When a company considers hiring someone with a violent history, its primary consideration is liability. No one wants to get sued for hiring someone with a violent past who then harms an employee or customer. The best thing you can do in your description, therefore, is to present the incident with as few details as possible and to discuss it as something that's as far removed from the person you are today as possible. By speaking in these terms, the employer will hopefully see the risk of incurring liability if they hire you as minimal. The following two descriptive responses both shy away from specifics and create distance. They each start off with our standard introduction:

"I'm glad you asked because I want you to feel comfortable about hiring me. My mistake involved a misdirected period in my youth that had a great deal to do with a lack of guidance at the time as a young person. I want to assure you that my offense occurred outside the workplace and had nothing to do with any employer, co-worker, or place of employment."

"I'm glad you asked because I want you to feel comfortable about hiring me. My mistake occurred almost a decade ago and, in so many respects, it was another lifetime ago. That lack of judgment had everything to do with a poor set of priorities at that time and nothing to do with any employer, co-worker, or place of employment."

The more professionally you carry yourself and the more removed your head and heart are from an incarcerated mindset or disposition, the more authentic and convincing you'll be as you describe yourself as being far removed from the person who committed that violent act.

Domestic Violence

Domestic violence doesn't scream "lawsuit" in the ears of most employers as loudly as other violent offenses do, because the term is saved for violence confined to the home. If there are no other violent incidences in your past, this offense allows an employer to deduce that risk in the workplace is minimal. Although, you should not downplay the seriousness of the offense in any way, being specific in this case may be beneficial, as it assures the employer that there is little liability at stake. Here is one way to shape the incident:

"I'm glad you asked because I want you to feel comfortable about hiring me. My mistake involved a bad marriage and a heated argument and me accidentally being inappropriate with my wife. The law says that even if your wife forgives you, the law doesn't until you've served your time, which is what I did. She's out of my life now, and the marriage counseling I received was very helpful in showing me where we went wrong."

Drug Offense

As stated earlier, most employers would rather take a chance on someone convicted of a drug offense than a violent offense. So, this is also a category where being specific could be useful.

"I'm glad you asked because I want you to feel comfortable about hiring me. My mistake was a non-violent drug offense. It was a regrettable time in my life that's so far removed from the clean and sober person I've become and the clean and sober life I live today that it feels like I'm talking about someone else that I used to know."

Theft

Theft is clearly a serious issue for companies, especially in those positions where merchandise could be a temptation and the opportunity exists to steal—if you were so inclined. It makes sense that no employer would want to invite theft by opening their doors to someone with a past that includes a history of burglary, robbery, larceny, or embezzlement. That being the case, staying away from specifics will probably serve your interests better than details would.

"I'm glad you asked because I want you to feel comfortable about hiring me. You know, Frank, I'll be the first one to call that mistake *down-right stupid*. It boiled down to me growing up in a neighborhood where hanging around the wrong people was an easy thing to do, which is unfortunately what I did. I made that mistake almost a decade ago, at a time in my life when I had no direction whatsoever. A lot—I say, again, a *lot* has changed since then—I have direction, now, I have focus, and I'm in possession of a healthy lawful life that I value a great deal. I have no intention of ever jeopardizing that."

"I'm glad you asked because I want you to feel comfortable about hiring me. Almost a decade ago, my life was off-track and I made some poor decisions. I want to assure you that my mistake didn't involve my previous workplace or employer. I have to say that the person I was then is so far removed from the person I am today that I don't even hold a resemblance to that person. It's embarrassing to even speak of that time in my life."

INCENTIVES

Once you've answered the big question, if you have a letter of recommendation from your previous employer, this is the time to pull it out.

"I think now might be a good time to give you a copy of a letter of recommendation that my last employer provided for me. It'll give you a sense of the kind of employee I am."

This would also be a good time to explain two federal programs the government offers as an incentive for employers who hire people with criminal records. To find out how your state handles the execution of both of these programs, go to the National Hire Network's Web site at www.hirenetwork.org/wotc.html.

If your crime involved theft of any kind, you should become very skilled at explaining the Federal Bonding Program. Some companies bond their employees as protection against employee theft, but, with a criminal past, it won't be easy to get you bonded on a typical company policy. The Federal Bonding Program provides the means for a company to get you bonded, and that can be reassuring to an employer who is considering hiring someone with a criminal record, especially if that record involved any kind of theft. The Federal Bonding Program issues fidelity bonds, which are basically business insurance policies that protect employers for, currently, a maximum of $5000 in case of theft, forgery, larceny, or embezzlement of money or property by an employee who's covered by the bond. It costs the employer nothing to obtain the bond and it goes into effect the first day you start work. Provide a copy of the information on this program to the interviewer at the appropriate time.

The second government incentive is the Work Opportunity Tax Credit. This credit requires ongoing congressional approval, but it provides employers a federal tax credit for hiring, training, and keeping individuals who were released from prison for a felony in the previous year (which means you only need to discuss the Work Opportunity Tax Credit if your felony is as recent as the past year). This credit can reduce an employer's income tax liability by, currently, as much as $2400 per qualified new worker. In addition, five states—California, Louisiana, Maryland, Texas, and Iowa—currently provide state income tax credits on top of the federal tax credit to employers who hire people with criminal records. The Work Opportunity Tax Credit program will provide an employer an added incentive for hiring you, although it's unlikely to convince them to hire you if they were set against the idea to begin with.

Many employers are unaware of either of these programs, so make sure you include this information if and when the conviction is discussed.

KEEP IT MOVING, THERE'S NOTHING TO SEE HERE!

Once you've answered the big question, you'll want to take the reigns and get the conversation moving again. One way to do this is by asking, "If I may ask, what's the company policy on hiring someone with a criminal record?" If they don't hire people with records, you know right away where you stand, which is good to know. If they have no formal policy in place, this is useful information, too, and a useful reminder to the interviewer that hiring you is at their discretion.

If the interview has gone well up to this point, this question reinforces the fact that whatever opinion of you the interviewer had prior to that discussion should still stand, and, that it's time to move the interview along.

If need be, take the reigns again and ask another question. There's no better way to change the subject or the direction of a conversation than with a good question that requires a little thought. The aim, of course, is to change, or divert, the course of the conversation without being obvious about the fact that you're attempting to change the subject.

That means you have to have a diversion question prepared and not leave it to chance. You never want to end up having to say something as transparent as, "How about this weather we're having?" or, "How 'bout those Celtics?" And, you won't successfully change the topic if you ask a question that can be answered with a "yes" or a "no," either.

Here are a couple of good diversion questions: "By the way, why has this position opened up?" Or, if that topic has already been covered, "By the way, I meant to ask, how would you describe the culture of the organization?"

THE BIG CONVERSATION:

This is what handling the big question looks like all strung together . . .

Ora: Chris, I see you've checked here that you have a conviction on your record. Could you tell me about that?

Chris: Sure. Actually, I'm glad you asked because I want you to feel comfortable about hiring me. My mistake occurred over a decade ago and, in so many respects, it was another lifetime ago. That lack of judgment had everything to do with a poor set of priorities at that time and nothing to do with any employer, co-worker, or customer. I think now might be a good time to give you a copy of the letter of recommendation my last employer provided for me. It will give you a sense of the kind of employee I am.

[Pause and hand over the letter]

If you don't mind me asking, what's the company's policy on hiring people in this situation?

Ora: Well, we really don't have an official policy on it. We just want good hard-working people.

Chris: Well, you definitely have a hard worker here, that's for sure. I'm also sure that's how all of my previous employers would describe me. Ora, are you familiar with the Federal Bonding Program?

Ora: I can't say that I am, what is it?

Chris: It's a federal program that enables me to get bonded for $5000 with a fidelity bond. The bond is provided at no cost whatsoever to the company. If you normally bond your employees or if it would make you feel more comfortable about hiring me, here is some information on it. You know I'm really excited about this position. I'm curious about why it opened up.

Ora: Oh, well, Margaret, who used to have this job, was moved to another department. We thought at first we were going to merge her position with another one but decided against it, so we're going to get a full-time person to take her old spot.

Chris: How soon are you looking to get someone in the spot?

Ora: We were shooting for the first of next month.

Chris: Great.

You notice how Chris smoothly transitioned from the conviction question back to a neutral topic that encouraged Ora to move forward? The importance of getting good at answering this question cannot be stressed enough. You don't want to miss out on a job you could otherwise have landed just because you couldn't handle the big question with finesse and diplomacy.

_____ *It's Your Turn* _____

At some point you'll need to take these ideas and write out a word-for-word script to help *you* answer the big question when it comes up.

1. Now that you know the objective, jot down a few sentences describing your mistake in a way that paints it in the best light possible. Remember to be honest without telling more than you need to.

2. Plug your script into the sample interview above, including an appropriate diversion question.

3. Recite the conversation aloud on a daily basis until you've memorized it and can say it on cue firmly, with conviction and without hesitation or a show of nerves.

THE POWER OF ATTITUDE

One last thing on this topic: attitude is everything. You paid the price for your mistake, so why should you pay again with the toll of shame in an interview? To be successful, for people to get the right scent from you, you have to embrace lawful living with your heart, your body, your mind, and your spirit. If you keep dancing in and out of the shadows you'll send the wrong signal. Your reform won't be visible, and it certainly won't be believed.

You want to send the signal that says, "It's okay to take me at face value; I am *today's* version of myself, completely and entirely." If you project this attitude, your interviewer will pick up on it and hopefully mirror it by taking you at face value. If, on the other hand, your attitude says, "I'm trying to see how this going straight thing works out for me," your interviewer will sense that as well, and you'll have sabotaged your own success. You'll end up with a self-fulfilling prophecy that sounds something like, "See? I *told* you no one would give me a chance. I'll have to go back to the same old same old."

Don't wait to get a job to embrace freedom and lawful living. Some people have their priorities mixed up; they say, "I'll get a job and then I'll get my act together," setting themselves up for failure. Embrace lawful living first, foremost, and unconditionally. Do this and an employer will have a hard time imagining they're looking at someone who could have ever committed a crime.

Chapter 7

THE END IS IN SIGHT

Typically, as the interview draws to an end, the interviewer will ask if you have any questions for them. Ideally, as discussed earlier, you've been able to ask questions throughout the interview, but this is your last chance to ask something as yet unasked. If you truly have no further questions because you've engaged in a good dialogue throughout the interview it's okay to say, "No, you've done a great job of answering all of my questions." If you've been unfortunately silent along the way, you absolutely *must* ask something now.

Two topics *not* to ask about are, and this is one of the biggest rules of interview etiquette, pay and benefits: *Never ask about pay or benefits.* Never. It may be tempting, especially if you're obviously closing in on the end of the interview, the interview seemed to go well, and the topics haven't been discussed yet. When you ask about pay, you're basically saying, "I know you're going to hire me, so why don't you just tell me what you're going to pay me." It's bad form. The same is true of asking about vacation days, sick days, and health or dental benefits. When either pay or benefits is brought up by the employer, it's a good sign. What *you* need to do is focus on giving a good interview and let the money follow.

The last phase of the interview is the close. You'll find that the more interviewers like you, the more specific they will be during this closing phase. You'll hear something along the lines of, "Well, the person in the position you would be replacing will be leaving in two weeks, so if we offered it to you we'd like you to start right away. Would that be possible?" Or, "Well, I just need to call on a few references here, your usual, standard stuff, and we'll be in touch." Or, "I'm going to talk to John, my partner, and we'll be doing a second round of interviews so he can meet all the people I like. That should happen some time next week."

Don't be surprised or feel threatened by the mention of a second interview. The higher up the food chain the position is, the more common a second interview is. Being asked to a second interview basically says, "I'm leaning towards hiring you; you've made the cut. Let's see what my partner thinks about you."

Unfortunately, one final hurdle might pop up. If you didn't fill out an application where the big question was asked and if it didn't come up during the interview and if the interview *did* go well, the close might include an off-handed, "Okay! So, the next step we take for applicants we're seriously considering is a round of background checks. Would that present a problem?" This is definitely a classic case of wrapping good news in bad news. The good news is that they like you enough to go to the expense and effort of doing a background check. Obviously, the bad news is that the check might disqualify you.

In this situation, try to calmly remember that not every company that runs background checks automatically rules out someone with a conviction, especially if the position doesn't involve handling money or obtaining a license or working in a field in which someone with a criminal record is legally barred. The best thing you can do is to be honest and straightforward, and then ask if this automatically disqualifies you from being considered for the position.

If the answer is "Yes," you can leave knowing that you gained valuable interview experience that you can draw from the next time out. In this case, continue to keep a good attitude. Don't let your discouragement show and don't become unprofessional in any way. Sometimes an interviewer who wants to hire you but is prevented from doing so by company policy may have a lead for you in another place or a sister organization. It pays to remain the professional you've trained yourself to be.

If the answer is "No, it doesn't automatically disqualify you" or, "We determine that on a case by case basis," then go through your script, just as you would have if the question had come up earlier.

If the company evaluates each case individually, the type of offense a person was convicted of is probably the deciding factor. In that case, the interviewer may ask you to be specific about the conviction: "What was the nature of your conviction?" is a nice way of saying, "What did you do?" If asked this specific question, simply name the conviction.

"Well, my mistake involved a theft that was unrelated to a workplace environment. Is theft a barred offense?"

If the answer is "no" then emphasize that this is something that's behind you now:

"I'm really glad to hear that because that's a life that I only see from my rearview mirror. I've turned my life around in every way, shape, and form. I now practice lawful living in every aspect of my life."

Once the interviewer has described the position and the company, has asked you all the questions they have prepared, and has answered your questions, the interview is very near its end. When the interview is over, don't linger. Just as the warm-up created an initial impression, the close leaves a final one—and you want that final impression to be a good one. Handle it professionally and exit gracefully. Remember, you're the good side-kick to the talk show host and when the show is over, it's over. A person who sits around, unable to sense that the interview is finished sends the message that they don't pick up well on social cues. This isn't the message you want to close with.

Once you hear the interviewer ask, "Do you have any *more* questions?" they are basically saying, "I'm done if you're done." If you're done, as well, a nice close is,

"No, I believe you've answered all my questions, and I just want to say, again, that I'm very interested in this job. I can really see myself doing good work here. Would it be okay for me to call next week to follow up?"

If the answer is, "No, I prefer to get back to people myself," don't take it personally; it's not even necessarily a bad sign. If they say, "Yes," ask for a business card if it hasn't already been offered to you. Make a point of noticing the interviewer's body language at this point and mimic it. As they start to gather their papers or put down their pen or push back their chair, you should begin to do the same: close your notepad or folder and put your pen away; when the interviewer stands, you should stand as well and prepare for a handshake.

The stock interviewer good-bye is something to the effect of, "It was a pleasure, Taylor. Thank you for coming in. We'll be in touch." Your stock response should be, "Thank you for your time, Janice. I look forward to hearing from you." Or, if you've been given the okay to call her next week, reiterate that with, "Thank you for your time, Janice. I look forward to speaking with you next week." Then turn and leave.

If a business card was never offered to you, pick one up from the receptionist on your way out or ask for the correct spelling of the interviewer's name and for the ZIP code if you don't know it. This information will be important for what follows in the next section.

Congratulations! You've gotten through an interview.

SEEING IS BELIEVING

Many athletes give themselves an extra edge before a game by visualizing the outcome they want to achieve when it's "go time." You might find envisioning an interview before you go on any real interviews to be helpful, as well.

To begin, close your eyes and take a few deep breaths. Once you feel relaxed, see yourself smiling and shaking hands with an interviewer. Watch as you respond with a "Thank you" to the offer of taking a seat, and notice that it's a straight-back chair. Adjust your clothes briefly, then leave them alone. Feel your feet being flattened to the floor, your back and buttocks pushing against the back of the chair, your eyes looking forward—your body alert, ready to go. Watch as the interviewer makes small talk and you respond appropriately.

As your imagined interviewer asks questions, take additional deep breaths and let them out with a smile and the words "It's mine; I have the job," while letting that excitement and good feeling travel through your entire body. Enjoy the sensation that comes with knowing you've responded perfectly to every question and you wouldn't have changed a thing. Experience the excitement that comes with knowing you hit the ball out of the park. Inhale this feeling and smile as you exhale. Don't hold back, really allow yourself to feel giddy. Now place your hand on your chest and repeat again, "It's mine; I have the job."

If you envision this on a regular basis, your body and mind will learn this manifestation of reality. It's been found that the mind doesn't really know the difference between thoughts that are real and thoughts that are vivid and repeatedly imagined, which is why visualization techniques are used by people who want to enhance their performance. So teach your mind and body this version of your interview. Envision it frequently, and this is the execution of an interview that you will manifest. Before you walk into the building for the real interview, take a deep breath, place your hand on your chest once more and repeat those words: "It's mine; I have the job."

Chapter 8

IT AIN'T OVER
TILL IT'S OVER

It's exciting to have your first interview under your belt. Be excited; be very excited, but don't be silly. And, silly would be slowing down in your job search. You should not slow your efforts until you hear the words, "You're hired!" No other words matter.

"We're looking to fill the spot right away and you're perfect for the position, Pat. In fact, you're the best person we've interviewed so far. You'll definitely be hearing from me." As good as this sounds, it's not the words you're waiting to hear: "You're hired."

So, the job search should continue.

Think about it for a minute . . . If they were *that* sure they wanted to hire you, why didn't they just do it on the spot? That certainly happens on occasion. The fact that they *didn't* hire you on the spot tells you that there's one more hurdle standing between you and the job. That means, if the hurdle is surmounted, you'll "probably" get offered the job—maybe; but, if the hurdle stands, you won't.

They may have been excited about you until the woman who came in right after you. They may have been ready to hire you until they called your previous employer and discovered that you're not as good of an employee as you painted yourself to be. They may have loved you but their boss may have preferred another candidate from the final pool. Who knows *what* happened between, "We love ya, we can't get enough of ya," and—silence. And that's the point: there's no way of knowing, which is why it's silly *and* makes no sense to call off the job hunt just because you got "the impression" you had the job.

There's nothing more frustrating than having to regain your momentum once you've lost it. Unfortunately, employers don't make a practice of calling everyone they interviewed to say they hired somebody else. This means you can waste a lot of time believing you have a job when, in fact, someone else already has your job. So repeat after me, "Nothing says I'm hired except the words, 'You're hired!'"

Except maybe, "You have the job," or, "Can you start on Monday?" Either of those will do just fine, too, just so we're clear.

THE FOLLOW UP

What you want to do while you maintain rational optimism after an interview is follow up. This is one last chance to make a good impression and to make yourself stand out in the crowd. Time is of the essence in this step. After the interview, you want to follow up with a thank you letter. If, during the interview, Ms. Grossi told you to call her "Barbara," then, in your salutation, use "Dear Barbara:" not "Dear Ms. Grossi:" or some other greeting. Here is an example of a thank you letter that would follow an interview:

Dear Barbara:

I want to thank you for taking the time in today's interview to provide a thorough overview of the pest control position you're seeking to fill. I am confident, and I hope you would agree, that I would be an asset to your team. I look forward to hearing from you on the matter.

The thank you letter should be short and sweet. If you drone on and on, it won't help your case; if you use it to beg and grovel, it will do you more harm than good; if, on the other hand, you use the letter above as an example, you'll demonstrate yourself to be the professional you are.

Just as with the thank you letters you wrote after the job fairs, for this thank you letter to be effective, *you must get it in the mail immediately*. Remember, the odds are good that Barbara will be interviewing several more people that week. If she gets your letter the next day, she should remember you; each day after that, however, with six or eight new people in her mind, her impression of you will grow foggier and foggier. So, for your thank you letter to have an impact, you need to mail it right away.

A thank you letter like this one is the simplest thing in the world to write. Look at it. We're only talking about a few lines of text. To not bother to write one means losing out on an advantage you could have given yourself. This is another example of a professional's behavior and another way to set yourself apart from all of the others who have never had instruction on how professionals go about a job search. Remember, the person who takes advantage of every opportunity to be effective ends up being effective. Don't let laziness cause you to miss out on this easy opportunity.

PROFESSIONAL REFERENCES

As discussed earlier, if an interviewer is serious about you, they will usually ask for three professional references. It's not a bad idea to carry this list with you to the interview so you can provide it, if and *only if* you're asked for it. Again, a professional reference is someone who has known you in a professional capacity, not the guy next door or your mother. A simple sheet of paper with the title "References for John Smith" will do just fine. Below that, list each person's name, job title, and phone number. That's all you need.

Some people are surprised to hear that the words of previous employers *can* have a negative impact on a potential new employer. Yes, it's true that no one wants to be sued, so employers aren't going to bad mouth the heck out of you. However, if someone is tight-lipped and chooses their words cautiously, someone who is used to doing reference checks will suspect a problem. That, then, triggers the single most important question an interviewer can ask in a situation where the employer isn't very forthcoming:

"If Carlos walked into your office tomorrow, would you hire him back?" There's no risk of a lawsuit with the honest answer to this question, but it sure says it all. The truth is that if his former employers had good things to say about Carlos, you wouldn't be able to shut them up.

If it's been a long time since you worked for a company that you would like to list as a reference, call the company—or drop by in person—and refresh your supervisor's memory. Let them know that you're engaging in a job search and that they will probably be getting some calls for a reference check.

If it's been a *very* long time since you worked there, odds are good that the person has since moved on. To find out, call the company and ask for your old supervisor. If the receptionist tells you they don't work there anymore, just ask, "So who would I talk to about a reference check?" When you get connected, introduce yourself and let them know when you worked there and under whose supervision and with what co-workers.

"I'm sure if you talked to Jim, my previous supervisor, or anyone I worked with at the time, like Maria, Frank, or Bob, they'd tell you how reliable and efficient a worker I was. By the way, are there any openings right now? At any rate, I just wanted to let you know that you'll probably be getting some calls for a reference check."

This conversation may be all the new supervisor needs to know. Chances are, instead of pulling up your old records, he will simply repeat back to the reference checker the words you just fed him: "Well, Larry worked here before I came on board with the company, but I understand he was reliable and efficient."

If you don't have a good reference out there, it can have a negative impact on your job search. Correct that disadvantage and create a relationship with a non-profit organization and some temporary employment agencies, as was described earlier.

Chapter 9

AVOID THE
FOUR TRAPS

You now know what it takes to engage in a successful job hunt. There's nothing holding you back but your own willingness to do what it takes. Implement the steps you've learned in this book and go for it. Just as 2+2+2+2=8, a strong resume + a killer cover letter + good interview skills + perseverance = employment, *without a doubt*. Begin your search and begin it immediately, but bear these four traps in mind along the way. And be willing to avoid them so that you don't impair your own success.

Trap Number One: I Have a Dream.

Getting a job takes sticking with the effort and never, ever giving up. It often also means being willing to start from the bottom. Some people wait and wait and wait for their dream job to come along, while turning down very respectable work because it's not that dream job. Meanwhile, those who accepted respectable work now have experience to propel them forward, money in their pocket, and a better shot at that dream job. On top of all that, they're at far less risk of going back to jail for doing something stupid and illegal for quick cash. As stated previously, you are three times more likely to go back to prison if you don't have a job. That's like playing Russian Roulette with three bullets in the chamber instead of one. Don't fall into this trap.

Your goal shouldn't be to find a dream job; your goal should be to find a starter job that you can upgrade. No one expects that the first house they buy will be their dream house, even if they're forty years old when they buy it. It's expected that your first house will be a starter home that you can resell for a nicer place in a few years.

This is the same logic that needs to be applied to a first job. It's extremely short-sighted to turn down jobs because they don't fit your image of positions for grown men or women with bills to pay and a family to feed. Sure a minimum wage job may not make a dent in your financial responsibilities, but what sense does it make to sit around talking about how you won't take any job unless it pays $25 an hour if your skills set or your education or your work history or your conviction prevents you from being able to command that kind of money right now? That kind of thinking leaves the door open for doing something stupidly illegal.

To be successful, you have to be realistic—not negative, but realistic. And you need to get realistic sooner rather than later because you don't want to miss the boat while you're waiting for a yacht. Go out there and get a job you're qualified for right now, then get the training it takes to command the money you want to make. If it's tough making ends meet, get a second part-time job. Get a couple of housemates. Sell things on eBay.

You could even start a part-time business on the side, but do it right. Secure your steady income first and foremost and then build your business in your spare time until it turns a profit and replaces your full-time income. Many people don't realize how long it can take before a business starts turning a profit from their investment—an investment that only another source of steady income is going to support.

One type of business that can be started with a fairly small investment and earn income in a learn-as-you-go environment is a multi-level marketing organization. These companies train you in building a business and marketing a product. Do a Google search at www.google.com and enter the words "multi-level marketing," or "network marketing," as the businesses are also called, and explore the possibilities. (By putting quotations marks around these search terms you should only retrieve results that include the use of both words together.)

The sky's the limit in what you can legally do to reach your dream job once you get some regular income coming in the door. So, don't give up your job search and don't give up your dream; just do it right.

Trap Number Two: Here a Job, There a Job.

Don't fall into the trap of giving up on the job search in exchange for doing little jobs here and there. Sure, you may be able to help your friend find people who are interested in refinancing their homes; and you may get $500 every time you find someone. But how often do you see that $500 payday? "Not often enough," is probably the answer. So be smart, get a legitimate full-time job, and help your friend out in your spare time.

Start thinking in terms of building a career. This means, rather than jumping from job to job, you stay somewhere long enough for it to be valuable to your resume. It means never quitting a job until you have a new job, and when it *is* time to move on it'll be to a better position in the same field. This is the kind of movement that will make your resume attractive and will allow you to move from the less popular functional resume to the more commonly used (and less suspicious) chronological resume that is only feasible once you have a solid work history.

Trap Number Three: Show Me the Money.

A very tempting trap to fall into is taking jobs just because the money is good when you know the position is impossible to maintain. For example, the job is so far away from home, especially on public transportation, that you have to get up at an unthinkable hour just to make it on time. How long do you think you can keep an arrangement like that up? Sure, you'll make good money for the five months you're able to keep the job, but then you'll be unemployed for as long as it takes to find new work—and, you'll fall behind on your bills again. In the end, you would have been better off making less money but making it consistently for a full year. If you don't think so, take a look at Jim and Sam who both took jobs in January.

Jim turns down a job that pays $8.50 an hour for one that pays $15 an hour. He doesn't like the work and the commute is long, but he figures how in the world can he turn down $15 an hour? Sam takes the $8.50 an hour job. Granted, it's not a lot of money, but he likes the work. Five months later, Jim can't take his job any more and he quits. He's unemployed for three months before he finds a new job and gets back to work. He ends up taking $8.50 an hour, just like Sam. At the end of the year, because Sam was realistic and took a position he liked where he knew he could stay, he's helped his resume with a work history that shows one year of employment with one company.

Jim, on the other hand, has done just the opposite. Chasing the money, Jim has hurt his resume with five months at one company, a three month gap, and four months at another company. Not only did Jim's decision to think short-term hurt his resume but it also hurt him in the pocket. At the end of the year, he realizes that between the five months he earned $15 an hour, the four months he earned $8.50 an hour, and the three months he earned nothing, he grossed a total of $17,440 for the year. Sam, who made $8.50 an hour for the full year, grossed $17,680. Also, since Sam has been with the company the full year, he got a nice holiday bonus check that Jim didn't get. *And*, while Jim continues to earn $8.50 an hour next month, Sam is now making $8.92 an hour because his year of employment qualified him for a 5 percent cost of living increase.

Fifteen dollars an hour may look better than $8.50 an hour on the surface, but if it's not a job you can do realistically for the long haul then learn from Jim and think twice before you blindly follow the money. Think long-term and you'll be better off for the long-term, think short-term and guess how long you'll be better off for?

How, then, do you plan for the long haul? If you know the type of work you would prefer doing, make a plan to get yourself there. Let's say for example your dream job would be to work for UPS or FedEx as a delivery driver. If that's the case, your first act should be to contact the human resource department of both these companies and find out what their policy is on hiring people with convictions. Don't give your name when you make this call, but make the call and get the truth from someone who knows, not a friend of your cousin's brother-in-law who knew someone who used to work there. If UPS hires people with your background, start building an attractive delivery driver's resume for UPS.

You do that by gaining some delivery experience. Any kind of delivery experience is going to look better than no delivery experience, so make that your goal. If it means taking a minimum wage job that allows you to gain valuable resume experience toward the bigger goal of earning much more money after paying your dues, doesn't it make sense in the long run? Sure, you may need to do other things as mentioned above to help make ends meet if you're making minimum wage but you know it won't be forever. You're climbing the rungs of the ladder in your desired field, and sometimes that means starting from the bottom rung—but that's okay.

Trap Number Four: Not Thinking Enough Moves Ahead.

Do you know why the average adult tends to always beat the average kid at a game of checkers or chess? Because an adult has the ability to think in terms of the next two or even three moves, whereas most children think only in terms of the one move in front of them at the moment. Don't fall into the trap of pursuing your career the way a child plays a board game. Learn to think a few moves ahead.

Starting at the bottom at a company can be the smart thing to do, but do the smart thing and start at the bottom at a company that has a middle and a top. If you take a job with a company that has no mobility, no place for you to advance to, then you'll be forced to leave the company in order to advance. Two fields that make this point well are the moving and carpet-cleaning industries.

Moving companies tend to have movers, estimators, and an administrative staff. The same is true for carpet-cleaning companies: they have carpet cleaners, estimators, and corporate administration. So, as a cleaner or mover, your most likely move up is to estimator, and then you're pretty much done moving up the ladder. Unfortunately, there are typically far fewer estimators than there are movers or cleaners so not everyone gets a chance at this advancement.

Where will you be a few years down the road at a company like this? Let's say you start at $8.00 an hour and you receive a 5 percent cost of living increase each year. Your second year, you'll earn $8.40 an hour; your third year, you'll earn $8.82; and your fourth year, you'll earn $9.26 an hour.

If, on the other hand, you start at $8.00 an hour with a company that has growth opportunity or has various arms to the company, it's quite common to go from $8.00 an hour to $9.00 an hour in just one move. Being willing to start from the bottom is the attitude that's going to make you successful, but play the game smart and think enough moves ahead so that you don't box yourself into a corner.

Any one of these traps can derail your efforts and ultimately impede your success. Unfortunately, sometimes friends or family encourage the pursuit of one if not all of the above traps, and you have to resist the urge to listen to them. Instead, try this: tell them you'll take their advice if they'll write you a check right now in case their advice proves faulty and you lose time or money following it, and watch their reaction. Assure them that you won't cash it unless and until their advice proves to be useless so "what's the problem?" At that moment, listen very closely to their response—it'll speak volumes. Thank them for their suggestions and then change the subject.

CONCLUSION

You have taken an important step by acquiring tools that will help you to execute a professional job search. You know how to customize resumes for their strength and appeal. You know what it takes to write a cover letter that will get your resume read. You know the dos and don'ts of interviewing. And you know not to stop until you hear the words, "You're hired!" You are now armed with everything you need to ensure that you will hear those words again and again as you carve out a career path.

Never forget that stereotypes and fears get broken down when enough people prove them wrong. Do your part to show employers that they've made the right decision in hiring someone with a record by being an excellent employee. The next record-carrying generation will either be hurt by the shadow you cast or will be able to stand on your shoulders and reach even farther because of the choices you make from this moment on.

APPENDIX 1: Online Job Search Sites

Popular Job Search Sites
www.craigslist.com
www.monster.com
www.hotjobs.com
www.careerbuilders.com
www.job-hunt.org

State Specific Job Search Sites

Alabama
www.jobsearch.org/al
www.newslink.org/alnews.html
www.pbjcal.org (Jefferson county only)

Alaska
www.jobs.state.ak.us
www.newslink.org/aknews.html
www.sled.alaska.edu

Arizona
www.jobsearch.org/az
www.newslink.org/aznews.html

Arkansas
www.jobsearch.org/ar
www.newslink.org/arnews.html

California
www.jobsearch.org/ca
www.newslink.org/canews.html
www.edd.ca.gov
www.caljobs.ca.gov
www.worksmart.ca.gov

Colorado
www.jobsearch.org/co
www.newslink.org/conews.html

Connecticut
www.jobsearch.org/ct
www.newslink.org/ctnews.html
www.ctdol.state.ct.us
www.Ctjobs.com

Delaware
www.jobsearch.org/de
www.newslink.org/denews.html
www.delawareworks.com

Florida
www.jobsearch.org/fl
www.newslink.org/flnews.html
www.floridajobs.org/onestop/os_job_search.html

Georgia
www.jobsearch.org/ga
www.newslink.org/ganews.html
www.dol.state.ga.us/js

Hawaii
www.jobsearch.org/hi
www.newslink.org/hinews.html

Idaho
www.jobsearch.org/id
www.newslink.org/idnews.html
www.idahoworks.org

Illinois
www. jobsearch.org/il
www.chicagojobs.com
www.newslink.org/ilnews.html
www.cityofchicago.org/careerworks

Indiana

www.jobsearch.org/in
www.newslink.org/innews.html
www. in.gov/dwd
www.indygov.org

Iowa

www. jobsearch.org/ia
www. newslink.org/ianews.html

Kansas

www.jobsearch.org/ks
www.newslink.org/ksnews.html
www.kansasjoblink.com (Scroll down to Quick Search to access job
    listings without registering.)

Kentucky

www.jobsearch.org/ky
www.newslink.org/kynews.html
www.workforce.ky.gov

Louisiana

www.jobsearch.org/la
www.newslink.org/lanews.html

Maine

www.jobsearch.org/me
www.newslink.org/menews.html
www.mainecareercenter.com

Maryland

www.jobsearch.org/md
www.newslink.org/mdnews.html
www.dllr.state.md.us

Massachusetts

www.jobsearch.org/ma
www.newslink.org/manews.html
www.boston-online.com
www.bostonworks.boston.com/worcesterworks

Michigan

www.michworks.org
www.newslink.org/minews.html

Minnesota

www.jobsearch.org/mn
www.mnworks.org
www.newslink.org/mnnews.html
www.mnwfc.org
www.iseek.org
www.mnworks.org/jsli.cfm

Mississippi

www.jobsearch.org/ms
www.newslink.org/msnews.html

Missouri

www.jobsearch.org/mo
www.newslink.org/monews.html
www.greathires.org
www.mo.gov/mo/working.htm

Nebraska

www.jobsearch.org/ne
www.newslink.org/nenews.html
www. nejoblink.dol.state.ne.us

Nevada

www.jobsearch.org/nv
www.newslink.org/nvnews.html
www.nevadajobconnect.com

New Hampshire

www.nhetwork.virtuallmi.com
www.newslink.org/nhnews.html

New Jersey

www.jobsearch.org/nj
www.newslink.org/njnews.html
www.nj.com/jobs

New Mexico
www.jobsearch.org/nm
www.newslink.org/nmnews.html
www.state.nm.us/clients/dol/metalist1.html

New York
www.jobsearch.org/ny
www.newslink.org/nynews.html
www.labor.state.ny.us
www.nytimes.com (Click on Job Market to access the job listings without registering.)
www.wnyjobs.com

North Carolina
www.jobsearch.org/nc
www.newslink.org/ncnews.html

North Dakota
www.jobsearch.org/nd
www.newslink.org/ndnews.html
www.sharenetworknd.com

Ohio
www.jobsearch.org/oh
www.newslink.org/ohnews.html
www.jfs.ohio.gov

Oklahoma
www.jobsearch.org/ok
www.newslink.org/oknews.html

Oregon
www.newslink.org/ornews.html
www.portlandrecruiter.com
www.emp.state.or.us/jobs

Pennsylvania
www.jobsearch.org/pa
www.newslink.org/panews.html
www.clpgh.org/locations/jcec

Rhode Island
www.jobsearch.org/ri
www.newslink.org/rinews.html
www.jobsinri.com

South Carolina
www.jobsearch.org/sc
www.newslink.org/scnews.html
www.sces.org

South Dakota
www.jobsearch.org/sd
www.newslink.org/sdnews.html
www.state.sd.us/dol

Tennessee
www.jobsearch.org/tn
www.newslink.org/tnnews.html

Texas
www.jobsearch.org/tx
www.newslink.org/txnews.html
www.ci.austin.tx.us
www.Twc.state.tx.us

Utah
www.jobsearch.org/ut
www.newslink.org/utnews.html
www.utah.gov

Vermont
www.jobsearch.org/vt
www.newslink.org/vtnews.html
www.vermontjoblink.com (Can use the Quick Search feature and avoid the Log in)

Virginia
www.jobsearch.org/va
www.newslink.org/vanews.html
www.careerconnect.state.va.us

Washington
www.jobsearch.org/wa
www.newslink.org/wanews.html
www.scn.org
www.work.wa.gov
www.workforceexplorer.com

Washington DC
www.jobsearch.org/dc
www.newslink.org/dcnews.html

West Virginia
www.jobsearch.org/wv
www.newslink.org/wvnews.html
www.wvjobs.org (Click on WV Jobs tab, then scroll down to Job List)

Wisconsin
www.jobsearch.org/wi
www.newslink.org/winews.html
www.dwd.state.wi.us/jobnet/mapwi.htm
www.wisconsinjobcenter.org

Wyoming
www.jobsearch.org/wy
www.newslink.org/wynews.html
www.wyomingworkforce.org
www.wyomingatwork.com

Ethnically Specific Sites

www.nul.org/employmentnetwork.html
www.ihispano.com
www.latpro.com
www.saludos.com
www.hirediversity.com
www.imdiversity.com

APPENDIX 2

Several cities are eliminating unnecessary employment discrimination in the hiring process for city jobs. In an effort to de-emphasize criminal histories for qualified city job applicants, San Francisco, Boston, and Chicago have removed the question "Have you ever been convicted of a felony?" from applications for city jobs. The question of criminal history will not be considered until further along in the hiring process in positions where the question is relevant.

Similar changes to city employment practices are under consideration or have been implemented in Minneapolis and St. Paul in Minnesota; Oakland, Alameda County, and the county and city of Los Angeles in California; Indianapolis and Marion County in Indiana; Newark, New Jersey; and the city and county of Philadelphia.

INDEX

U
using last names, 74, 124

V
victimless crime, 109
violent offenses, 107, 109-110
visualizing the interview, 120
volunteer work:
    benefits of, 49
    construction skills, 49
    how to obtain, 48
    listing on resume, 49
    office skills, 49

W
Work Opportunity Tax, 112
writing pen, 77, 93
www.HelpAfterPrison.com, 29, 42, 65

ABOUT THE AUTHOR

Pam Hogan knew she had found her calling in 1994 when she became a self-development trainer specializing in conflict management and effective communication. It wasn't until five years later however, when she began training individuals who had served time in prison that she knew she had found her passion.

To satisfy her desire to help those still locked behind bars, Pam produced the video course *Successful Employment and Lawful Living through Conflict Management* in 2006. This prisoner reentry program, now in use in jails and prisons across the country, helps prisoners gain the skills they'll need for a successful return trip home.

In an effort to expand her reach even further, in 2007 Pam launched *HelpAfterPrison.com,* the first membership Website of its kind. This site makes it possible for members to acquire computer training, self-development, and employment resources.

Although Pam has never served a day behind bars herself, she has made her professional mission serving the needs of those who have. This book is one more contribution to that mission, and she hopes it serves you well.

A Personal Note from Pam

CONGRATULATIONS on taking such an important step in
securing your freedom and
embracing lawful living.

In support of your effort, please accept my
special FREE gift to you.

Go to www.HelpAfterPrison.com
and click on *From Prison to Paycheck* for your gift.

Quick Order Form

Fax Orders: 415-586-0870

Telephone orders: Call 888-739-2973 toll free.
                        Have your credit card ready.

Email Orders: Orders@AcommunityPress.com

Postal Mail Order: Community Press, P.O. Box 31667
                        San Francisco, CA 94131, USA
                        Telephone: 415-333-4594

PRICE: $19.95

Sales Tax: Please add 8.5% for books shipped to California addresses.

Shipping

U.S.: $5.00 for first book and $2.50 each additional.
International: $10.00 for first book; $6.00 for each additional (estimate)

Payment: ❏ Check   ❏ Visa   ❏ MasterCard

Card number:_____

Name on card:_____ Exp. Date: _____

Bulk Orders
We offer substantial discounts on bulk orders to correctional facilities.
Call our correctional facilities production department at 888-222-8189
for pricing.